This book is dedicated to the Lord Jesus Christ and to the family He put me in. While my parents have done more than I can ever thank them for, some of their specific interests and gifts had a direct influence upon the writing of this book. My parents set a good example of active learning about the real world. Dad enjoyed military history and keeping up with world news; Mom enjoyed the museums and other cultural attractions of Chicago, where we lived. Though we did not travel far, we enjoyed some of the scenic attractions in the Midwest: Wisconsin Dells, Indiana Dunes, the Apostle Islands, and Black River Falls. My parents also made it possible for me to visit Washington, D.C., with my junior high class. The gift to me of a Viewmaster reel on the Seven Wonders of the World when I was ten first stirred my interest in this particular subject.

I would also like to thank my other relatives, all of whom encouraged me in various ways. The slides of Thailand shown by my cousin David Tank interested me in travel. I also fondly remember my first trip alone, as a boy of about fifteen on a bus to Ohio to visit the Osbornes. I later visited on occasion the Gobens or the Tanks on my trips north. With gratitude for their influence, I hope this book will encourage my parents and relatives. May they see the Lord's providence everywhere.

Contents

Introduction

The Seven Ancient Wonders

The Seven Technological Wonders

The Seven Archaeological Wonders

The Seven Architectural Wonders

Figures

THE SEVEN WONDERS OF THE WORLD

You will notice immediately that there are thirty-five wonders of the world in this book. This is because there are five groups of seven wonders. The ancient wonders have been described from the times of ancient Greece; however, all but one have been destroyed. What are the wonders of the world now? The technological wonders include the seven great engineering feats of the twentieth century. The archaeological wonders consist of the world's greatest ruins, all of which were unknown to the ancient Greeks. The architectural wonders were built before the twentieth-century boom in technology, but they do not lie in ruins. The seven natural wonders are the greatest sights in all of God's creation.

None of these wonders is included in more than one category. The Great Pyramid of Egypt, an ancient wonder, could also be considered an archaeological or architectural wonder. However, the Great Pyramid has been acknowledged by all as an ancient wonder of the world, and its inclusion in a second list cannot add to its recognition.

What is a wonder of the world?

Of course, a wonder of the world must inspire wonder in the observer. By looking at the choices of ancient writers, one will recognize several principles that guided their selections. Such strict criteria insure that the place instills profound wonder in observers from all lands.

1. Local
2. Beautiful
3. Superlative
4. Majestic
5. Unique
6. Historic
7. Classic

SEVEN WONDERS
OF THE WORLD

A wonder of the world must be *local,* that is it must be a specific location that you can visit. Moving vehicles—whether they be satellites such as *Sputnik I* or ships such as the *Queen Mary*—fail to qualify since they do not remain at a specific place. Similarly, small objects such as the Hope Diamond and the Mona Lisa can be sold or loaned and moved between museums too easily. Continent-spanning wonders, such as the U.S. interstate highway system or the Sahara Desert, are not specific places either. All wonders nominated by ancient writers were specific places; not until modern times did writers include some inventions.

A wonder of the world must also be *beautiful.* Beauty was important to the ancient Greeks, and no drab structure was ever considered as a wonder of the world. The Chicago Sewer System is a marvel of engineering and technology, but no sewer system ranks among the wonders of the world. In contrast, the Taj Mahal has a charm and beauty unsurpassed in the world.

A wonder of the world must be *superlative.* Its size should not only be enormous and imposing but also set an unsurpassed record in its class. Size alone does not make something a wonder, but size is important. Of the many beautiful ancient statues worldwide, the Greeks selected only two, and both were incredibly large: the Colossus of Rhodes and the Statue of Zeus.

A wonder of the world must be *majestic.* Sometimes the large or the beautiful may seem majestic, but majesty goes beyond these. Majesty describes elegant things fit for a king, dignified and stately, grand and magnificent, regal and splendid. Archaeologists at Herculaneum dug through lava from the eruption of Vesuvius and uncovered a private house. The house was important because it contained a cross, proving that Christianity had reached Italy before the eruption of A.D. 79. No matter how important the house was during its era, it lacks the majesty of a castle, temple, or cathedral and cannot be called a wonder of the world. Peter Clayton, an archaeologist, explained that all seven ancient wonders exhibited great size, beauty, and majesty, thus producing awe and wonder in the observers.

A wonder of the world must be *unique* in design. It should stand out as being in a class by itself. The Hanging Gardens were one of a kind; nothing similar had ever been built. The Dutch Dike system provides a modern example.

A wonder of the world must also be *historic*. Every wonder of the world has an intriguing history. Many also pique curiosity and provoke a sense of mystery and adventure. Wonders of the world captivate the mind with thoughts of who built the place, who inhabited it, why it was built, and what happened there. Lachish is an interesting ruin in Israel, but the interesting items found there have been dispersed to museums around the world. A visitor to Lachish finds only a city-sized mound of dirt. Nothing reminds him of the interesting history; Lachish has lost too much of its wonder to be a wonder of the world. Each of the seven ancient wonders of the world has a history so intriguing that the ancient writers often devoted more space to its history than they did to its appearance!

The ultimate test for a wonder of the world is whether it is the *classic* example in its field. To be a classic, it must serve as an established model or enduring standard. The Grand Canyon is certainly the classic canyon, while St. Peter's Basilica is clearly the cathedral against which all others are measured. While Chartres Cathedral in France is very beautiful, none would argue that it rivals St. Peter's as the classic cathedral.

Unfortunately, to become a classic requires a consensus of public opinion, and such opinion must remain constant. Certainly universal acclaim of people from all time periods, all nations, and all religions is final proof that a site belongs among the wonders of the world, but this is rarely possible. Even the seven ancient wonders were disputed until the Renaissance. Since no ancient writers included the Sphinx (though they saw it new and unweathered), no later writers have acknowledged it either. People are naturally proud of sites in their own country, but a wonder of the world must receive recognition from abroad. Most religions honor their holy sites, but very few holy sites can impress people of other religions as well.

Who selects the wonders of the world?

The list of ancient wonders was first published around the time of Christ and has been confirmed by many writers since. It is the only category of seven wonders that is undisputed. However, even in ancient times some writers questioned a few places on the list. For more on these disagreements, read the Introduction to the ancient wonders of the world (p. 3).

As for the other types of wonders, no two books on modern or natural wonders in this century (see the Bibliography) ever agree completely. The lists in this book were made by comparing choices of other writers and testing them against the requirements for wonders of the world listed above. Most of the earlier books include technological wonders that are now outdated; however, many of their categories, such as dams, skyscrapers, and suspension bridges, are still important. The most recent ones have had little opportunity to stand the test of time, so check an almanac for newer constructions.

In the end, it is not the person who compiled the list who is important, but whether his list passes the test of universal acclaim. The goal of each writer on the subject is to capture the seven undisputed masterpieces in each category. He hopes to make selections so obviously great that no one will disagree. The compiler must avoid provincialism and maintain a worldwide scope; he must not include too many familiar places from his own country, and he must research diligently so that he does not miss any candidates that were recently found or built. As you read this book, your opinion is important. If you disagree with one of the selections of one of the seven wonders, you reduce its universal acclaim. Please defer final judgment until you consult Appendix 2, which explains why certain famous places were excluded.

What makes the seven wonders of interest to Christians?

Everything created reflects its creator. Christians can see God in all the things He made. The ancient wonders highlight God's sovereignty over history as well as provide background for New Testament times. The technological wonders remind men that God gave man dominion over the earth. The archaeological wonders, which lie in ruins, show that God eventually brings judgment on sin and idolatry. His patience yields to His justice when the iniquity of a culture is rampant. The architectural wonders show that God is merciful and patient with sinners. The natural wonders clearly reveal God's eternal power and Godhead. As a final emphasis, the Epilogue discusses some wonders in Jerusalem that proclaim the redemption God provided for man in Jesus Christ.

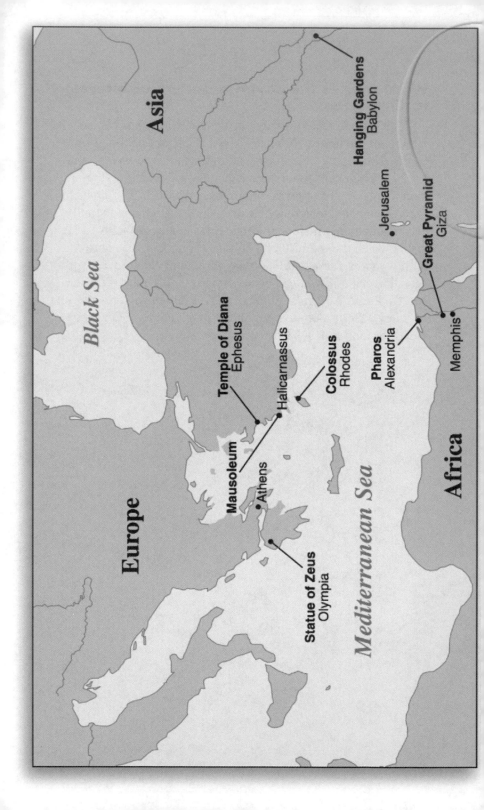

Seven

ancient

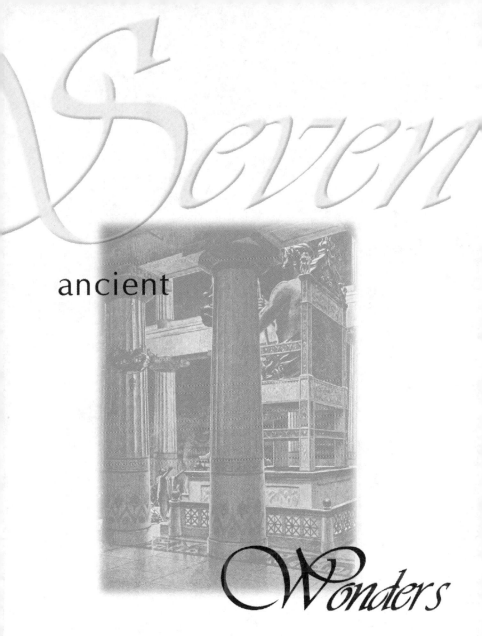

Wonders

7 The Seven Ancient Wonders

Herodotus wrote the earliest descriptions of many of the ancient wonders of the world in the fifth century B.C., though he did not call them "wonders of the world." Callimachus of Cyrene wrote a short work entitled "A Collection of Wonders in Lands Throughout the World." This is perhaps the only work to be written while all seven wonders still stood, between 270 and 226 B.C. Later, Philo of Byzantium wrote the first book devoted to the subject, *De Septum Orbis Spectaculis,* ("The Seven World Spectaculars"). Antipater of Sidon, Diodorus, Strabo, Pliny the Elder, Gregory of Nazianzus, and Bishop Gregory of Tours also mentioned the seven wonders of the world. All seven wonders appear on the map below.

Many ancient writers disagreed about the seventh wonder, the Pharos. In place of the Pharos, Antipater of Sidon listed the Walls of Babylon, which were more massive than the walls of any other fortified city of his day. Others replaced the Pharos with the Altar of Pergamum, the Palace of Cyrus at Ecbatana, the Capitol at Rome, or the city of Thebes.

Early Christian writers did not dispute the Pharos but instead rejected the pagan Temple of Diana and the Statue of Zeus. They replaced these pagan sites with the Temple of Solomon and Noah's Ark. The early Christians did not recognize that they could appreciate beautiful architecture without condoning the pagan purpose of the building. If we were free to select our own seven ancient wonders, the library at Alexandria would very likely be included; however, by the time of the Renaissance, the seven listed above had become standard.

The ancients selected the greatest sights that could be seen in the world. The lists excluded Stonehenge and the Great Wall of China since England and China were beyond the known world. The Palace of Minos (Knossos) on Crete had burned one thousand years before and was only a legend to

them. The Colosseum at Rome had not yet been built. Since
Noah's Ark is not a destination available to tourists, the
Christians should not have included it either. The Temple of
Solomon was a more serious omission, which is discussed in the
Epilogue.

All seven ancient wonders display God's sovereign purpose.
The famous pyramids proclaim to all that Egyptian culture goes
back as far as the Bible claims it does. The Bible stories of
Abraham, Isaac, and Joseph in Egypt are factual. God decides
which individuals and nations rise and fall. The Bible records
how God raised up Nebuchadnezzar, made him king of a vast
empire, and gave him great riches. The fact that the whole
world recognized his Hanging Gardens as a wonder of the world
testifies to his riches. The Greek Empire provided an international trade language and transportation system. The Pharos
testifies to the importance of shipping. The Greek culture and
language prepared the world for the inspired New Testament
Scriptures, but God's patience with Greek idolatry eventually
ceased. The destruction of the statues of Zeus and Helios
(Colossus of Rhodes) proves it. In fact, the Ephesians falsely
worshiped Diana for thousands of years, but in God's sovereignty, even the site of the temple had been lost. Evidence of
God's sovereignty is seen frequently in this chapter.

"The king's heart is in the hand of the Lord, as the rivers of
water: he turneth it whithersoever he will" (Prov. 21:1).

 ## THE PYRAMIDS OF EGYPT

"Maybe this thing *is* just a monument," said Caliph
Ma'mun. "The whole thing seems solid." The Arabs took over
Egypt around A.D. 650, but the new caliph of A.D. 818 refused
to believe that the pyramid was solid, even though everyone
said so. He lost no time in commanding his men to dig an entrance. They had bored a hole about thirty feet up the north

side of the pyramid and only twenty-five feet below the original entrance. After a long, slow going, the Caliph was almost ready to give up. Suddenly, the entire pyramid reverberated with the crash of a boulder deep within. "Wow! We shook something loose. There must be rooms somewhere."

They broke through at a junction of tunnels. They could look above and behind them at a short passageway to the original entrance, now blocked. In front of them two passages led into darkness, one upward and one downward. First, they crawled through the four-foot high passage downward. Almost immediately as they descended, the tunnel changed from stone to earth, and they could tell that they were beneath the pyramid. They descended over a hundred feet and peered into a larger room. The empty room, the size of a mansion's bedroom, eleven feet high, forty-eight feet long and twenty-seven feet wide, doused their hopes of riches. In the center of the crypt, they noticed a deep hole. The Caliph ordered, "Throw a torch down there." Lit by the flickering light, they saw the bottom of the forty-foot shaft, but it was empty like the crypt.

"Let's explore the ascending passage." As they climbed back up toward the junction, they noticed a hole in the roof. They stood at the bottom of a vertical well rising into the gloom, far too steep to climb. When they returned to the junction, they climbed into the ascending tunnel but saw that the passage was blocked by a huge boulder. They dug around the boulder and continued up to another junction. This time, three passages confronted them, one going straight down, one straight ahead, and one continuing to ascend.

The black hole gaped below them and seemed to swallow a thrown torch. "This must be the top of the other hole, but we can't explore it without ropes." The horizontal passage continued one hundred feet on the level and ended in a larger chamber with a pointed roof. They dubbed it the Queen's Chamber because Arab tombs used pointed roofs for queens. Small vents ascended from the chamber, one to the north and one to the south, but both were choked with debris.

The third passage, ascending, widened immediately. "The King's Chamber must be near!" The grand gallery, 28 feet high, ended after 155 feet. At the top, they passed through an antechamber into a large room. Silence and millions of stones surrounded them as they paused in the heart of the pyramid. The largest room, with two more small air vents, was not empty. An impressive granite coffin, seven and a half feet long, stood in the center. The caliph sauntered toward it and looked in. "Empty!" He screamed in anger, "It's empty! All the treasures are robbed, even the coffin lid and the mummy."

The caliph had spent much money to get into the tomb in hopes of treasures. Though disappointed, he was correct. The pyramid did have passages inside. They found five small chambers above the King's Chamber before they left. The pyramid had also once held great riches. Each pharaoh made his own pyramid as a tomb. Egyptians knew that life does not end at death, but they did not understand that after death there is no need for earthly things. They mummified the bodies to help preserve them and put everything the king might want in the tomb with him, from personal valuables and jewels to food and hunting equipment, and even furniture and musical instru-

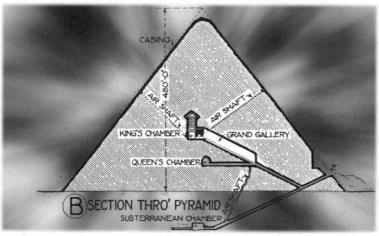

Passageways inside the Great Pyramid

ments. The riches, however, had been stolen perhaps two thousand years before.

In the tenth century, when the Arabs built their new capital, Cairo, they used the ruins

The Great Pyramid and the Sphinx

of Memphis and some of the pyramids as sources of stone for building. However, removing stones from the pyramids took too much effort, so they removed only the top stones of the Great Pyramid. They did remove almost all the outer casing of limestone, so today when viewed close-up the pyramid looks like a very steep staircase for giants. The top of a neighboring pyramid (Khafra) still retains its casing at the top, which shows how smooth the pyramids would have looked when they were first built.

Khufu (or Cheops to the Greeks) built the Great Pyramid, and the neighboring pyramids were built by Khafra and Menkaure. The Sphinx, with the face of a man and the body of a lion also stood nearby, but the pyramids dwarfed the sixty-foot high Sphinx. While there were over seventy-seven pyramids around Cairo, the Great Pyramid surpassed them all in size. It originally stood 482 feet high, and even after the Arabs removed the top stones, it still stood 449 feet high. The Great Pyramid was the tallest structure in the world for over two thousand years until the Pharos was built. After the Pharos toppled, the pyramid became the tallest structure again, even though by then it was thirty feet shorter. It remained the tallest building until the completion of the cathedral spire at Cologne in 1880.

The Great Pyramid covers a square area of 755 feet on each side, which is larger than a city block. The accuracy of the right angles at the corner still surprises modern engineers. The pyramid required two million blocks of stones, many weighing four tons, or as much as a hippopotamus. Some weighed fifteen tons, and the granite blocks above the King's Chamber weighed forty-five tons.

The laborers wanted to build elaborate tombs for the pharaohs because they worshiped the pharaohs as gods. According to Herodotus, one hundred thousand men labored for twenty years to build Khufu's pyramid. Researchers have found the barracks for four thousand full-time year-round stone masons and engineers. The rest of the laborers worked only during the flood season, when they could not farm their land.

Teams of several hundred men tilted each stone block so that a wooden sled could be slipped under it. They hauled each block from the quarry to the pyramid with long reed ropes, crossing the Nile River on a ferry boat. One man walked in front of the stone and poured water to help the stone slide along on the slippery ground. At the pyramid, they pulled it up long gradual ramps to get it in place and adjusted its position using wedges, which could be inserted from either side by tilting the stone again. Adding or removing wedges would raise or lower the stone several inches. After positioning the topmost block, the laborers worked from the top to the bottom, covering the whole pyramid with white limestone to fill in the steps for a smooth surface. At the same time, they removed the ramps. Priests led the procession that deposited the mummy of the king and his possessions. On the way out, a worker triggered huge boulders in the Grand Gallery, that came crashing

Stones of the Great Pyramid

down the incline and plugged the passage. The worker descended the vertical shaft as best he could, perhaps with help of a rope and a

small chamber
halfway down.
When he reached
the bottom and
pulled down the
rope, there would be
no way to return up
the steep chute.
Finally, he crawled
up the descending

passage, where he released another boulder to block the outside entrance.

The pyramid's fame rests on its size, accuracy, inner mysteries, and age. What is the oldest thing in the world? The oldest living things are the bristlecone pine trees, which grow at high elevations in Utah, Nevada, and California. Botanists date these gnarled, twisted trees using tree rings, and they think the Methuselah Tree in California is the oldest, about 4,600 years old. If so, it began growing not long after the waters of the Flood receded. Egyptian history suggests that the Great Pyramid was built around 2600 B.C., which makes the Great Pyramid as old as the bristlecone pines, and the oldest man-made structure on earth! Unlike the Methuselah Tree, which required visiting America, the Great Pyramid has been known by historians since it was built. Today, it is the only one of the seven wonders of the ancient world that still stands. The Great Pyramid and two smaller ones are at Gizeh, near Cairo, the modern capital of Egypt.

At the pyramids, history lives. Napoleon visited the pyramids in 1798. The Arabs saw the pyramids when they conquered Egypt around A.D. 650. When Joseph and Mary took Jesus to Egypt, they may have seen the Great Pyramid. Herodotus saw the pyramids which had presided from a distance over the battles of kings for nearby Memphis: first King Esarhaddon of Assyria in 672 B.C., next King Cambyses of Persia in 525 B.C., and then Alexander the Great in 332 B.C.

Moses, being part of the royal court of Egypt, must have seen the pyramids around 1500 B.C. Around 1880 B.C., Joseph became the second ruler over Egypt under Pharaoh (Gen. 41:41-43) and would certainly have been familiar with the Great Pyramid. His father Jacob and all his brothers came to Egypt later and saw the pyramids as the family moved from the capital to Goshen. Abraham visited Egypt with his wife Sarah around 2100 B.C. and could have visited the pyramids. Some think that Job 3:14 refers to the pyramids built for the burial of the Pharaohs. Perhaps even Noah lived long enough after the Flood to hear about the pyramids (Gen. 9:28).

THE HANGING GARDENS
OF BABYLON

Queen Amytis dropped a scarf and stepped aside from the path of the charge. She had never seen a matador, but she had learned the hard way how to dodge a charging bull. Amytis watched her bull paw at the scarf and spoke soothingly, "My king, why must you act like a bull? Where is your right mind?" The bull's attention turned from the scarf to the nearby flowers, and he began grazing on the imported irises. "You always did have expensive tastes, but thank you for this beautiful garden. You have built for me a mountain in the desert with terraces of trees and flowers and grasses imported from all over the world. I love the flowers, for they remind me of the mountains at home in Medea and the royal court of Cyaxares, my father. The cool of the garden refreshes me from the heat of Babylon. Still, I wish your madness would leave. You don't need me now, and the palace is lonely."

The queen's gaze wandered from the mad king, a prisoner in his own garden high above the city where none would see him. From her position she could look out across Babylon. She glanced at the moat around the garden below and the royal palace nearby. The Euphrates River flowed through the city, and in the distance Amytis admired the great ziggurat, the Tower of Babel, topped by the Temple of Marduk, covered in gold and inlaid with blue-glazed bricks. Earlier she had enjoyed the sunrise, which made the blue and gold shine across the city. She recalled too the gold statue of Marduk and the gold furnishings inside the temple. The parks and buildings spread before her as far as she could see. She knew the prince could run the empire, and she feared no threat of invasion. Babylon's impregnable wall comforted her.

No other city had walls like Babylon. Its two walls stood eighty feet apart, the outer wall twenty-five feet thick and the inner wall twenty-two feet thick. The space between the walls was filled in almost to the top to combine the two walls into one huge structure so wide that four-horse chariots could pass each other as they drove around on the top. The huge wall ran fifty-six miles around the city. There were one hundred gates through the wall, but the Ishtar Gate dazzled the eye with its splendor. From this gate the grand processional avenue ran to the Temple of Marduk, lined on both sides every sixty-four feet with sculptures of lions. The avenue was seventy-three feet wide—as wide as an eight-lane-expressway.

Motion brought her attention back to the bull. She should not have let her thoughts wander so long in his presence. She heard her name, "Amytis." The king stood erect and spoke, "Amytis, my mind recalls strange deeds. What has happened?" Startled, the queen gathered her thoughts, "Nebuchadnezzar, my lord, are you sane? You have been crazed for seven years, living outside with the flowers and beasts of these gardens, away from men and eating grass as an ox. Let us go up to the Temple of Marduk and give thanks for your sanity."

"No, Amytis. Your words remind me of my sins. This is not from Marduk but the God of Daniel. When I boasted, 'Is not this great Babylon, that I have built,' God judged me and said, 'The kingdom is departed from thee. And they shall drive thee from men, and thy dwelling shall be with the beasts of the field: they shall make thee to eat grass as oxen, and seven times shall pass over thee, until thou know that the most High ruleth in the kingdom of men, and giveth it to whomsoever he will. (Dan. 4:29-37). We must ask Daniel how to give thanks to his God."

Nabopolassar had joined forces with Cyaxares to defeat Nineveh in 612 B.C. and had arranged the marriage of his son, Nebuchadnezzar, and Amytis at that time. In 605 B.C., Nebuchadnezzar had conquered all of Palestine at the Battle of Carchemish. When he returned and took the throne, he probably began building the gardens, which he finished around 600 B.C. In 594 B.C., he quelled a revolt, and in 585 B.C. he began his thirteen-year siege of Tyre, finally bridging the channel to the island by filling it with rocks. He conquered Egypt about 568 B.C. and perhaps made his boast when he returned victorious. If so, his forty-two-year reign from 604 to 562 B.C. ended shortly after his sanity returned.

Herodotus recorded the size of the walls that Nebuchadnezzar built and the twenty-six tons of gold used in the Temple of Marduk. Diodorus Siculus told of the garden's foundations, stone slabs supported by arches eighty feet high. The term *hanging* comes from these arches, which supported terraces or balconies that seemed to float above the city.

Diodorus also explained the water system of hydraulic pumps from the well underneath the garden. Strabo described the various levels of terraces linked by wide stairways and the continuous slave labor that powered the pumps that kept the garden watered. Quintus Curtius mentioned trees in the garden up to twelve feet in girth.

The wide terraces mounted pyramid-style to three hundred feet in height. From each terrace, covered deeply with earth, grew large fruit trees shading grassy meadows. Profusions of fragrant flowers lined the meadows, their scents wafting into the cool and luxurious royal chambers. The whole structure covered a square area, similar in size to a quarter-mile track surrounding a collegiate football field.

The garden design included rooms nestled under the archways, royal staterooms at the upper levels and grain storage in the basement. The rooms were kept cool by building in stone and planting shade trees. Having no stone, Nebuchadnezzar had to import large quantities at great expense. Engineers had to design the first hydraulic hand pump to carry water to the top for the trees. No similar pump has been found in ancient ruins. To avoid water seeping into the rooms, the engineers put layers of reeds, pitch, and lead between the layers of stone ceiling.

Sennacherib destroyed Babylon completely in 689 B.C. Yet Esarhaddon ordered its rebuilding only ten years later. After rebuilding the Tower of Babel, the city reached the height of its prosperity under Nebuchadnezzar. After several of his sons and sons-in-law murdered each other for the throne, his son Nabonidus ruled for three years until 553 B.C. At that time, Nabonidus decided to live in Arabia and left his son Belshazzar to rule as his delegate in Babylon. In 539 B.C., Belshazzar, being second over the kingdom, made Daniel third in the kingdom (Dan. 5:29) because he had revealed the meaning of the unknown handwriting on the wall. The next day though, Darius the Mede conquered Babylon. How did he get through the impenetrable walls? According to legends, he diverted the Euphrates River and followed the riverbed.

In 482 B.C., when Babylon revolted against Persia, Xerxes destroyed the Temple of Marduk and melted down the gold. In 331 B.C., Babylon surrendered to Greece, and Alexander the Great died in the palace. He had planned for Babylon to remain his capital, but the city declined shortly after the capital moved elsewhere. By 200 B.C., if they were not already rubble, the garden plants would have died without slaves running the water pumps.

Ruins of Babylon's Ishtar Gate

The city had been laid waste for centuries when a German archaeologist, Robert Koldewey, excavated Babylon from 1899 to 1917. He marvelled at the remains of the three-hundred-foot tall Tower of Babel, the Temple of Marduk, the forty-foot-high Ishtar Gate, and the city walls. Koldewey read all the ancient writers and knew that the only structure with stone foundations was the Hanging Gardens of Babylon. In 1903, near the palace, he found a stone ruin of fourteen rooms with arches for ceilings. He immediately thought of the Hanging Gardens and soon uncovered a well with three shafts for hoisting buckets of water. He imagined the slaves who pushed the handles of the hydraulic pump night and day to bring water to the top terrace. The dimensions also matched the historical records, and he knew he had found the famed gardens.

Ruins of the Hanging Gardens

Perhaps the city will be rebuilt one day, but the Bible guarantees that eventually Babylon "shall be desolate for ever" (Jer. 51:61-62) for "Babylon the great is fallen" (Rev. 18:2).

THE STATUE OF ZEUS (JUPITER) AT OLYMPUS

Alexis surged into the lead as they raced around the track. Alexis had raced in the Olympics four years ago but had not won. He had trained hard for the last ten months and hoped that he had a good chance to win this year, 432 B.C. He refocused his thoughts on the race as he saw the halfway marker. Spectators lined both sides of the one-stadion course (630 feet). The cheering escalated, alerting him that an opponent neared. The sight of his main rival bounding ahead drew from him more speed than he thought he had. The two raced neck and neck toward the finish, urged on by the cheering crowds. The crowds went wild as Alexis barely edged out his opponent at the finish line. He listened as heralds called out his name, his father's name, and his city. He received his victory wreath—a token of the honor he had won for himself, his family, and his city.

Alexis recalled the preliminaries of the first day, when each athlete testified that he was eligible to race as a Greek citizen and vowed to obey the rules. Each umpire vowed to refuse bribes and judge fairly. He remembered the pentathlon on the second day. Alexis had not won because, although he had excelled in the footrace and broad jump, he had not done well enough with wrestling, discus, and javelin. Though defeated, he had watched the other runners to learn about his main competitors. Alexis had relaxed afterward during the chariot races and other horseraces in the Hippodrome. There were no events on the third day, which always fell on the full moon and was devoted to sacrifices to Zeus. That was yesterday, and the crowds in the Sacred Grove had discouraged him from entering the temple. Alexis had never heard of any other religion, and he wanted to thank his god for victory. This year, though, there was another reason that he could hardly wait to visit the Temple of Zeus, the chief god of the festival.

After the other footraces, including one in full armor, Alexis took a break before the wrestling, boxing, and freestyle fights. Tomorrow was the last day of these Eighty-sixth Olympics, the first of which were in 776 B.C. He knew tomorrow would be filled with celebrations and preparations to return home, so he took this chance to visit the temple. He pushed his way between the musicians, tumblers, vendors, and past the embassies of various city-states toward the Sacred Grove. Though his worship of the false god Zeus never satisfied his inner need, he very much wanted to visit the temple this year.

Alexis scanned the many temples and statues that he re-

membered from his last Olympics, including the Temple of Hera and the statue of Hermes by Praxiteles. Of course, the Temple of Zeus stood in the center; its 210-foot length and sixty-foot width made it the largest temple at Olympia. Libon of Elis, the architect, had finished the temple in 456 B.C. after fifteen years of work. Columns supported the roof, and paintings adorned the front and rear. He could see the paintings of Pelops and Oenomaus preparing for their life-and-death chariot race as well as small paintings of six of the twelve labors of Hercules. He remembered the other six labors depicted on the rear along with the

Ruins of the Temple of Zeus at Olympus about 1870

scene of the Centaurs battling the Lapiths. Though beautiful, the temple had stood vacant for over twenty years, waiting for the sculptor Phidias to make a statue of Zeus. After Phidias finished the Parthenon, he had moved to Olympia and set up a workshop. Since the previous year he had finished his last great work of art; these Olympics offered most visitors their first chance to see it. In spite of being tired from the race and the August heat, Alexis increased his pace, eagerly climbing the steps and passing among the pillars of the temple.

Alexis grew reverent. Zeus sat on a cedar throne with a high back, covered with gold and with sphinxes for armrests. Though seated, the statue towered forty feet high, several stories above Alexis. If Zeus could have stood up, his head would have gone through the roof. Besides the size, the statue commanded attention for its beauty. A gold mantle decorated with lilies and animals draped over the statue's ivory skin. The golden sandals rested on a golden footstool. Gold also formed its tunic, and precious stones served as eyes. His left hand grasped the royal scepter of gold topped by an eagle, and his right hand supported the small winged figure of the goddess of victory, Nike, also in gold and ivory. Both Zeus and Nike wore olive-wreath crowns such as Alexis had received. The statue depicted Zeus as strong and noble as Homer had described him, with "swarthy brow and flowing locks," beard and long mustache, just the way Alexis would have wanted him to look.

For several centuries, the statue stood under the care of Phidias's descendants. Due to the damp climate, they had to oil the ivory parts regularly to keep them from cracking. One legend says that Emperor Caligula, around the time of Christ, tried to transport it to Rome and to substitute a sculpture of his own head for Zeus's; but when his workmen touched the statue, loud laughter echoed forth and thunderbolts destroyed their ship. In the second century A.D., Pausanias visited Olympia and left the only remaining description of the wonder. In A.D. 267 barbarian invaders damaged many buildings in Olympia, but apparently not the Temple of Zeus. In A.D. 385, the list of Olympic winners ends with the 291st Olympiad. Eight years later, Emperor Theodosius I, a Christian ruler of Rome, abolished the games as pagan.

What happened to the statue? Some accounts say it toppled and crumbled in an earthquake, while others claim that Theodosius II smashed it to pieces in A.D. 426. In 1875, a German expedition found fragments of the statue and a sunken pool for oil, which lends credence to these accounts. Perhaps Theodosius II finished what the earthquake had begun.

THE TEMPLE OF DIANA (ARTEMIS) AT EPHESUS

"Great is Diana of the Ephesians!" roared the mob that filled the amphitheater. Demetrius, a silversmith, made small copies of the temple for individuals to buy. He had more concern for his material gain than for the message of truth that Paul preached. The interest shown in the message of Jesus Christ scared Demetrius because it seemed to threaten his prosperity. Demetrius appealed to civic pride to create an uproar, and the shouting continued for three hours, even though most of the people did not even know why they were shouting (Acts 19:32). Finally, the town clerk calmed the mob by reminding them that Roman rulers would demand a reason for this riot and that Paul had not robbed their temple.

Roman coin depicting the Temple of Diana

In A.D. 1090, the Turks conquered the region of Ayasalouk, where Ephesus had stood. Grassy swamps covered the whole area, and when the Turks asked to see the fabulous temple, the villagers answered, "What temple?" No one even knew that one of the seven wonders of the world had once stood nearby. John Turtle Wood led an expedition of the British Museum in 1863 to find the Temple of Diana. Bandits, lack of funding, few workmen, and a broken collarbone from falling off a horse plagued his efforts. Wood knew both the biblical account and the other ancient writings. Pausanius said, "It surpasses every structure raised by human hands." Pliny the Elder, who died in the eruption of Mt. Vesuvius that buried Pompeii in A.D. 79, called the temple "the most wonderful monument of Grecian magnificence." Pliny described its beauty: sculptures by Praxiteles adorning thirty-six of the columns, a roof of cedar planks, doors of cypress, and the statue of Artemis inside also made of wood. From Pliny, Wood also knew that the Greeks built the temple on swampy ground to make it less prone to earthquakes. From other sources, he knew that the temple had been outside the city walls but not far.

Wood dug seventy-five pits and many trenches, enough to find many interesting ruins, but not the temple. He had not known that the river had silted up the harbor, causing the city to become less important and eventually causing the city to be several miles from shore. Thus, some of his earlier excavations only convinced him that the temple did not lie between the city and the sea. In 1864 he sent crates of the sculptures to the museum to satisfy his impatient sponsors. In 1865 an assassin mistook Wood for the British ambassador to Turkey and stabbed him within an inch of his heart. The wound healed, and five weeks later he searched again. Officials and landowners complained, brigands attacked, he found a dead body in one building, and American tourists pestered him. Year after year, he found tombs, city gates, a theater, and a gymnasium, but no temple.

In 1868 he struck a huge road made of limestone and rutted by chariot wheels. He ran out of money after digging along the road only five hundred yards. By the time the museum agreed to fund yet another year, his digging would have interfered with the local harvest. When he could dig again, he found a stone wall, and the British Museum permitted him one more year. The pressure mounted; he had to find it this year. Turning to dig along the wall, he immediately found inscriptions in Latin and Greek saying that Emperor Augustus had built the wall. From Tacitus, he knew that this wall, built in 6 B.C., stood close to the temple, and he followed it hundreds of feet both ways. Money ran out with no success.

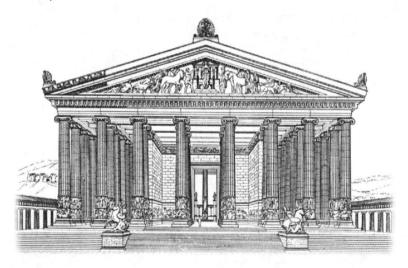

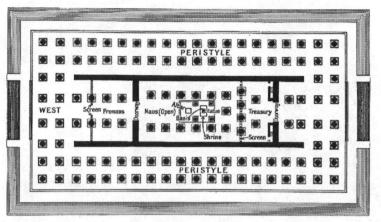

Floor plan of the Temple of Diana

Because the inscription offered hope, the museum extended its offer one more year. Battling swamps, snakes, and scorpions, Wood kept digging. On the last day of the year, a workman struck stone twenty feet down in a hole. Ignoring fevers and chills, Wood rejoiced in 1870 when he had found the temple. He took five more years to clear out the muddy field containing the temple foundations. The size staggered him—an ancient building much larger than a football field—342 feet by 163 feet and resting on an even larger platform. Its 127 columns had soared eighty feet into the air—higher than a ten-story building. By comparison, the Parthenon in Athens seemed small, being only 230 feet by 100 feet and sporting only fifty-eight columns, each thirty-four feet high.

Wood's crew found several complete columns and sent them to the British Museum, where they remain on display. Fifteen men worked fifteen days removing each column from the pit, and when they reached England, a team of twenty horses moved them one by one. Sculptures decorated the columns, and Wood also found chips of temple paintings. He could not afford to dig much deeper, but he saw that the temple had been built on top of the ruins of an earlier temple.

D. G. Hogarth led a second expedition of the British Museum in 1904. While the location of the temple was now

Ruins of the Temple of Diana

known, the swamp had reclaimed the site and tangles of reeds ten feet high grew from the muck. As they dug into lower layers of the temple, they hit springs that flooded the dig. Every day they pumped the site dry and dug while wading in the water as it immediately began to rise again. This time, they found evidence of five temples, and they suspected that earlier temples had been made of wood and had rotted away, leaving no trace. They also found part of the altar and many coins, figurines, and jewelry that had been given as offerings. Hogarth, like Wood before him, hoped to find the statue of Diana that must have stood at the altar, but neither expedition found any trace of it.

Ephesus, founded as a Greek colony around 1087 B.C., had a shrine for worship of Artemis. The image of the goddess, which her followers claimed had fallen from heaven (Acts 19:35), may have been a meteorite shaped somewhat like a woman. Artemis, the Greek goddess of the hunt, armed with her bow and arrows, later became identified with the Roman goddess, Diana. However, the Artemis of the Ephesians, though also identified with Diana, was a fertility goddess and not a patron for hunters.

About 660 B.C., barbarians from Cimmeria invaded the city and destroyed the temple. The Ephesians rebuilt the temple, but another invasion left it in ruins again. The city commissioned the architect Chersiphron to design a new one, and he finished the third temple by 600 B.C. In 550 B.C., King Croesus, famous for his wealth, conquered Ephesus and destroyed the temple again. In a show of goodwill, Croesus paid for a new fourth temple four times larger than the old one. The new temple was about the size of a football field, one hundred yards by fifty yards. More than one hundred stone columns in a double row supported the roof. Four sculptured Amazons, one each by Pheidas, Polycleitus, Kresilas, and Phradmon, won the contest to decorate the triangular pediment above the front columns. Cyrus of Persia obtained the entire empire of Croesus. On the night that Alexander the Great was born in 356 B.C., Herostratus, a madman, burned down the temple.

By this time, two hundred thousand people lived in Ephesus and its walls extended for eight miles. Trade from all over the world came to the harbor and made the city very rich. The people gave to the rebuilding effort and hired the sculptor Scopas of Paros to direct the construction of the fifth Temple of Artemis at Ephesus. Legend says the enormous task took 120 years to finish. Theodorus, the engineer, designed the temple even larger than before and decorated it with paintings by Apelles and sculptures by Praxiteles. In 333 B.C., Alexander the Great liberated Ephesus from Persian control and offered to fund the remaining work if his name could appear on the dedication stone. The Ephesians tactfully refused, saying, "How can one god dedicate a temple to another god?" Alexander, flattered at being called a god, left happily. God struck Herod dead for accepting such flattery (Acts 12:22-23), and perhaps pride went before the fall for Alexander as well.

About 323 B.C., the temple was finished, and Antipater of Sidon wrote, "I have gazed on the impregnable walls of Babylon along which chariots can race and on the Zeus by the banks of the Alphaeus. I have seen the Hanging Gardens and the Colossus of Helios, the great man-made mountains of the lofty pyramids and the gigantic tomb of Mausolus. But when I saw the sacred house of Artemis, the others were overshadowed."

Two centuries later, in 133 B.C., Ephesus came under Roman control. The Romans enlarged the city again, and the population neared its peak by the time the apostle Paul visited around A.D. 52. In A.D. 262, the Goths burned Ephesus and its temple. By then, the religion of Artemis was dying, but the worshipers of Artemis rescued the marble idol of their goddess. St. John

Chrysostom demolished the last remains of the temple in
A.D. 401, but before the final destruction, the worshipers buried
the idol under the floor of the city hall to protect it from destruction by Christians. The archaeologists found the temple
hidden in the swamp but missed the idol hidden in the middle
of the city that they saw every day. The idol remained under
the ruins of city hall for fifteen hundred years until an Austrian
archaeologist discovered it in 1956.

 # THE MAUSOLEUM
AT HALICARNASSUS

Heartbroken, Queen Artemisia could not cry anymore. She
loved Mausolus her husband, King of Caria. His death in 353
B.C. had almost wrung the will to live from her. He had ruled
the province of the Persian Empire for thirty-four years, conquered Rhodes and Lycia, and built a new capital at
Halicarnassus. The queen looked out her window across the
city at the wide boulevard and the Temple of Apollo that her
husband had built. In fact, he had built for her the brick and
marble palace in which she sat. She wept at the memories.
"Why did his energetic and powerful reign have to end?"

"Servants!" Artemisia continued without pause, "Send messengers throughout all Greece to obtain the finest artisans. We
shall build the king the most splendid tomb in the world." The
servants departed, but a messenger remained behind. "My
Queen, I bring you evil tidings that the city of Rhodes rebels
against your rule and sends ships to attack the capital here."

The emergency occupied Artemisia's thoughts. She recalled
the king's secret fort and canals at the east end of the harbor.
Artemisia hid her fleet at the fort. When the ships of Rhodes
arrived, they docked unhindered and entered the capital tri-
umphantly. The queen's fleet quietly entered the main harbor
and towed the ships of Rhodes out to sea. With the troops of

Rhodes stranded at the capital, Artemisia's soldiers manned the enemy ships and sailed to Rhodes. The people of Rhodes welcomed their ships only to find them filled with the queen's troops! Rhodes surrendered to the wise queen's tactics.

Soon the architects Pythias and Satyros, and sculptors Bryaxis, Leochares, Scopas, and Timotheus assembled with famous bronze-workers and other craftsmen. Work began on the tomb, but the queen's grief returned. Rulers of Caria married their own sisters by custom, so the queen mourned the loss of Mausolus, her king, her brother, and her loving husband. The queen wasted away and died only two years after her husband. Nevertheless, the craftsmen finished the monument for her.

Tomb of Mausolus

Alexander took Halicarnassus in 334 B.C. and marvelled at the Mausoleum, tomb of King Mausolus. The 140-foot high white marble tomb gleamed brightly from a hill above the harbor. Alexander entered the gate in the stone wall of the courtyard and saw the lion sculptures guarding the steps up to the platform. A low wall ringed the platform and supported figures of gods, goddesses, and warriors on rearing horses at each corner. Sculptured reliefs of Greeks fighting Amazons decorated the main chamber of the tomb, which was 126 feet long by 105 feet wide. Upon this chamber stood thirty-six columns that supported a pyramid of twenty-four steps. Statues of the king and queen in a four-horse chariot, twenty-five feet tall, crowned the whole. Alexander decided to let it stand.

Paul may have seen Halicarnassus and its Mausoleum when he sailed past Ephesus. The monument remained intact until

about 1400 when an earthquake rocked it, and the chariot crashed to the court-yard below. In 1402 the Knights of St. John of Jerusalem built a crusader castle overlooking the town, then called Bodrum. They used the Greek city for building material, including the top of the Mausoleum. In 1522 they repaired their castle walls for the attack by Sultan Suleiman. They ground and burned the remaining marble blocks to get lime for plaster. They robbed the interior art and sarcophagi. The Turks, however, drove out the knights.

In 1846 with permission, the British Museum collected former Mausoleum reliefs and sculptures from the castle. Ten years later, Sir Charles Newton excavated the Mausoleum site and found building fragments and sculptures of Greeks, Amazons, a chariot wheel, a chariot horse, and the royal couple. They identified the ten-foot statue of Mausolus from coins bearing his image. Some thought the damaged female figure was Athena, but the goddess would have been carved larger than the king and the devoted queen would have commissioned the artists to depict herself with her husband. The museum created the Mausoleum Room to display these relics of a tomb so famous that all large tombs are now called mausoleums.

THE COLOSSUS OF RHODES

"Punish Rhodes!" said King Antigonus of Macedon to his son Demetrius. The merchant fleet that made the small Greek island of Rhodes its home port had provided transportation for some of the armies of Ptolemy of Egypt in his attack on Macedon. Now, Antigonus wanted revenge.

In 305 B.C., Demetrius arrived for battle. The men of Rhodes sank two enemy ships, but the enemy warriors outnumbered their entire population. They fell back as Demetrius—with forty-thousand trained soldiers—captured the stone breakwater that protected the harbor. From the refuge of their walled city, the men of Rhodes fired catapults in defiance, but huge battering rams manned by one thousand soldiers soon broke through the city wall. Concentrating their forces at the breach, the defenders fought valiantly while others worked furiously to repair the wall. They tore down the temples of their own gods for stone.

The people of Rhodes knew that almost two hundred years earlier, Greeks had bravely fought the Persians, defeating a larger force at Marathon and giving their lives at Thermopylae. The stories of such bravery inspired them as the Alamo inspires Americans. As the battle wore on, women offered hair for bow-strings and prepared ammunition

Legendary view of the Colossus straddling the harbor

all night. Slaves received weapons and the promise of freedom if Rhodes won.

The alarmed citizens of Rhodes watched 3,400 Macedonian soldiers push a nine-story tower on wheels toward the city walls. Each level of the tower had a water supply for dousing fires and hatches for firing catapults. Rhodes launched a surprise attack by night and set the siege tower ablaze by bombarding it with flaming missiles. The tower retreated for repairs, and soon soldiers pushed the rebuilt tower forward. This time Rhodes diverted its water supply outside, and the tower stuck in the mud.

Months passed, and news of the siege spread across the known world. At Rhodes, however, food ran out, and hunger and disease spread. After holding out for a whole year, the brave citizens sensed the end but would not surrender even if it meant death. One day, a lookout cried, "Ships on the horizon!" Ptolemy of Egypt had remembered Rhodes. Demetrius retreated hastily, leaving his siege engines behind.

The people of Rhodes celebrated and decided to commemorate their success. They hired Chares of Lindos to erect a statue of Helios, the sun god, whom they worshiped and whom they believed had protected them during the battle. Chares, the

Probable reconstruction of the Colossus

sculptor, made the statue from bronze by melting down the deserted siege engines that the Macedonians had left behind.

The statue, too large to lift into place on the large base, had to be erected in sections. Chares cast each section separately and fit it into place. He kept the proportions correct by matching the large sections to a scale model. Iron scaffolding and stone blocks gave support on the inside. To get to the higher sections, workers mounded up dirt around the statue to successively higher heights so that a ramp spiraled up around the outside. In 282 B.C., after twelve years of labor, the workers removed the dirt to reveal his masterpiece.

Indeed, the Statue of Helios was a masterpiece. It was a work of art of gigantic proportions. Those who saw it called it the most beautiful and perfect human form ever imagined. Just before it was finished, legend says that Chares committed suicide when he found a single flaw. The statue faced the rising sun for fifty-six years, but an earthquake toppled the giant in 226 B.C. Helios broke at the knees and fell on his face as helpless as the false god Dagon, which broke its hands when God toppled it on its face (1 Sam. 5:2-7).

While the statue stood above the harbor, travellers sailed from across the known world to see it. In fact, the Colossus of Rhodes was so tall that the term *colossus*, originally used for any statue, came to be reserved for huge statues. It still ranks as one of the tallest statues ever made. Ancient writers recorded the dimensions of the statue, including its seventy-cubit height. Though cubit lengths varied, modern research concludes that Helios stood about 110 feet tall from head to toe—about the same height as the Statue of Liberty—with an additional eighteen feet if the white marble base is included. The chest of the Colossus, sixty feet around, is larger than many bedrooms. The statue's thickness measured eleven feet at the thigh and five feet at the ankle. The statue's thumb was so large that very few grown men could reach their arms around it.

No one knows how the colossus looked, but coins and images from the period usually showed Helios with a crown of rays such as adorns the Statue of Liberty. The statue of the sun god appropriately faced the rising sun, and robes probably draped over the left arm, hanging to the ground to cover a supporting column. Late drawings showed the right hand shielding the eyes, extended, or holding aloft a torch (or the sun), but these are doubtful. Some even presented the statue with one leg on each side of the harbor so that ships would enter the harbor by sailing between them. However, with a quarter-mile wide harbor, neither the statue's size nor its construction method supports the idea. Instead, it probably stood on the breakwater at the harbor's entrance or higher up at the Temple of Helios.

For over 875 years, the statue remained where it had fallen. When Paul and Luke visited Rhodes (Acts 21:1), they could have viewed its broken limbs and peered into its vast interior caverns. Greek and Egyptian engineers failed to repair it.

When the Arabs conquered Rhodes in A.D. 654, they shipped the fragments to the mainland. The general sold them to a Jew from Emesa, who bought and sold scrap metal. He carted away three hundred tons of bronze on nine hundred camels and sold it to makers of common household trays and lamps—an end fitting for a false sun god.

THE PHAROS (LIGHTHOUSE) OF ALEXANDRIA

The world's tallest structure towered over swarms of people. Crowds of shoppers and businessmen bustled through the busy streets. Students from all over the world attended the famous university and researched in the world's largest library. Ships of all sizes stood in the harbor. A canal linked the seaport with the large river system. Was this New York City? Washington, D.C.? No, it was Alexandria, Egypt, and tourists traveled across the known world to see the tallest building in the world—the lighthouse of Alexandria.

Sailors first sighted the beacon from one hundred miles away, a whole day before reaching Alexandria. The smoke of the lighthouse by day and the flame as bright as a star by night guided ships into the harbor. The fire burned day and night throughout the sailing season. Perhaps Apollos returned on such a ship to the city of his birth (Acts 18:24).

Approaching the port, Apollos discerned three distinct tiers. As he walked to the end of the breakwater, the beauty of the white marble, the hundreds of windows and statues, and the incredible size combined to provoke a sense of wonder. Inside, he marvelled at the many government offices, stables for three hundred horses, and the barracks for the military garrison. He walked up the gently sloping spiral ramp, wide enough for chariots to pass him carrying fuel for the beacon. He exited the ramp onto the first balcony above the square-shaped first tier of the building. Here, from the refreshment stands, he bought drinks, fruits, and even lamb on a stick similar to the way modern vendors sell corn dogs. As he entered the second eight-sided tier, he saw the chariots unloading the fuel onto hoists to be pulled up to the top. The stairway narrowed so much that he could not turn around, but then he exited onto the balcony above the second tier. The observation deck offered a spectacular vista across the city, the sea, and Lake Mareotis.

After climbing the final narrow ladders in the topmost cylindrical tier, Apollos arrived at the highest balcony. Here workers continually piled fuel on the brazier to keep the huge fire going and adjusted the enormous glass lens that magnified its brightness. He recalled the stories he had heard of how the lens could be focused on enemy ships twenty miles away and cause them to burst into flames. The heat prompted him to descend to the previous deck.

Now Apollos noticed the statue of Poseidon, the Greek god of the sea, standing on the topmost dome. Seeing the Greek god turned his attention to the three hundred thousand souls lost in sin in the city below. He felt the Holy Spirit prompting him to preach, and the great orator turned all his skills to preaching, "Repent from your sins and be converted, knowing that Christ died for your sins."

Once, Alexandria had been a little fishing village, called Rhakotis. Alexander the Great had chosen the town, situated

Reconstruction of the Pharos based on archaeological finds showing all the tiers

on a neck of land dividing marshy Lake Mareotis from the Mediterranean Sea, for his city. Alexander's architect Deinocrates of Rhodes laid out the city with its two harbors. The breakwater, over three-fourths miles long (seven stadia), stretched from the shoreline to the small island Pharos and protected the seaport. A canal connected the freshwater harbor with the Nile River twenty miles away. This permitted trade with Greek cities as well as with the major cities of Egypt but avoided the Nile delta with its flooding and silting problems. Deinocrates laid out a beautiful city with palace, gardens, parks, a zoo, museum, library, and the tomb of Alexander, who did not live to see it.

Ptolemy succeeded Alexander over Egypt, and when the new city was finished, he moved the capital from Memphis to Alexandria. The city produced linen, glass, and papyrus, and with its two harbors for trade, it imported ivory and gold from Africa; oil, wine, figs, and honey from Greece; and spices and cloth from India. The city grew quickly, and Ptolemy commissioned the architect Sostrates to build a lighthouse at the end of the breakwater. Sostrates finished the work around 270 B.C., during the reign of Ptolemy's son. Even with the free slave labor, the building cost eight hundred talents of gold, approximately $500,000 in today's currency. The lighthouse soon became known by the name of its island, Pharos.

Sostrates used white marble blocks fused together with molten lead for the building except for the foundations, which he made out of glass. Because the foundations would have to withstand the sea, he experimented with various building materials to determine the most durable. He threw equal weights of gold, silver, copper, lead, iron, glass, brick, stone, and others into the sea. When he hauled them out, only the glass had not weathered. He used the sea, however, to his own ends. A plaster plaque dedicated the lighthouse to Ptolemy as expected, but eventually the sea wore the plaster away to reveal this inscription underneath: "Sostrates, Son of Dexiphanes of Knidos, on behalf of all mariners to the savior gods." This referred to the Greek gods, which had displaced the old Egyptian gods after Alexander's conquest.

Ptolemy II required every traveler to give his books to the library, where a scribe would make a copy of the original book for the traveler. This policy spurred the growth of the library, which became the largest in the world. Alexandria later came under Roman control, and Julius Caesar visited in A.D. 47. He fell in love with Queen Cleopatra, but a mob killed him three years later in a riot against Roman rule. When Mark Antony's bid for power failed, Cleopatra committed suicide. By the time of Christ, three hundred thousand persons, not including slaves, lived there. Growth continued until A.D. 616, when the Persians took control. Thirty years later the Arabs captured it after a fourteen-month siege, and they moved the capital to Cairo in the tenth century.

Artistic conception predating archaeological finds

Some say an earthquake destroyed the lighthouse in A.D. 796. Others say that Constantine sent a spy in A.D. 850 to the royal court in Cairo who convinced the caliph that the lighthouse covered buried treasure. The Arabs tore down the top stories of the lighthouse before they realized the trick, but they could not repair the tower, and the great lens had broken. The latter legend highlights the rivalry between Constantinople and Alexandria. Perhaps the legend that Alexandria could use the great lens to spy on people in Alexandria arose as a rebuttal.

Idrise, a Moorish scholar from Spain visited Pharos in 1115. He recorded measurements of all three tiers, proving that no levels had been destroyed or dismantled. He said that the lighthouse stood three hundred cubits high or equal to about one hundred statures of men. While cubit lengths varied, the mention of human statures suggests that the lighthouse was at least 500 feet high and probably between 575 and 600 feet high. Confirming these measurements, another source gives a measurement which converts to 590 feet. Fifty years later, another Moorish scholar also described the lighthouse. By then, while all the tiers still stood, the beacon no longer functioned and had been replaced by a Moslem mosque.

Around 1375 an earthquake did destroy even the lowest tier of Pharos. In 1480, Kait Bey, the sultan of Egypt, used the ruins and foundations to build his own fortress, which still stands. In 1962 a young Egyptian went spearfishing and found statues, columns, and a sphinx underwater. The museum curator guessed that the large statue was Poseidon from the top of the Pharos.

The fame of the Pharos showed in other ways too. Even though smaller lighthouses had preceded Pharos, such as the one at Sigeum (Troy), Pharos set the standard for all later constructions. Roman architects used Pharos as a model for lighthouses at Ostia and Carthage. Also, several languages, such as Latin, Spanish, Italian, and French, borrowed the name *pharos* as the word for lighthouse.

Great Pyramid

Freighter in the Panama Canal locks

Itaipu Dam

Akashi-Kaikyo Bridge

CN Tower

Channel Tunnel Train

Stonehenge

Great Zimbabwe

Angkor Wat

Easter Island Statues

Grand Canyon

Gateway Arch

Cliff Palace at Mesa Verde

Borobudur

Palace of Versailles

Machu Picchu

Taj Mahal

Dome of the Rock

Neuschwanstein Castle

Great Wall of China

The Serengeti

Iguaçu Falls

St. Peter's Basilica

Mt. Everest

Erik's Glacier (Eiriksjökull) in Iceland

Frozen Niagara inside Mammoth Cave

Afsluitdijk (see Dutch Dikes)

El Castillo and the Temple of the Warriors at Chichén Itzá

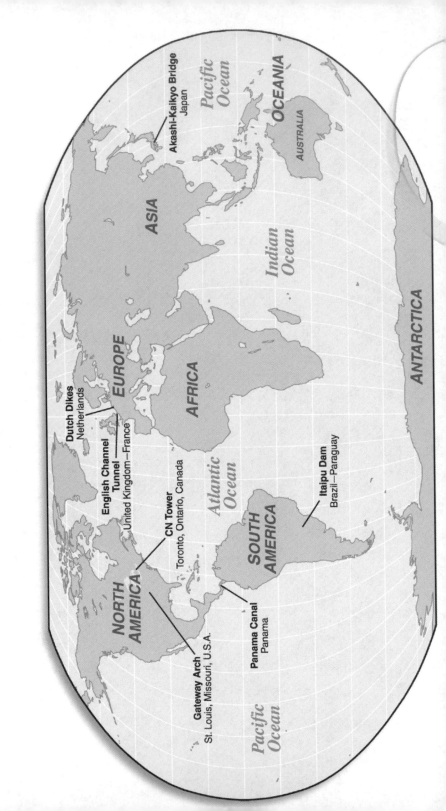

Seven

technological

Wonders

7 The Seven Technological Wonders

Confronted with a list of seven ancient wonders of which only one remains standing, the obvious question is "What are the seven modern wonders?" Lists of the seven modern wonders of the world typically include the longest suspension bridge, the largest dam, and the tallest skyscraper. Compare the four lists of modern wonders below. You can see that modern technology plays a major role in these lists. In fact, this chapter will include only wonders of technology. Wonders dating before the twentieth century will be postponed until later chapters. All four lists reflect many major advances of the twentieth century, but since these lists date between 1959 and 1970, many of the wonders listed have been far surpassed.

Leonard Cottrell	Robert Silverberg	Lowell Thomas	Viewmaster
Empire State Building	Empire State	Empire State	Empire State
Grand Coulee Dam	Grand Coulee Dam	Hoover Dam	Grand Coulee Dam
Golden Gate Bridge	Transbay Bridge	Shibam	Mackinac Bridge
Snowy River	Panama Canal	Taj Mahal	Taj Mahal
Jodrell Bank	UN Building	St. Peter's Basilica	Chartres Cathedral
Calder Hall	Washington Monument	Angkor Wat	Angkor Wat
Sputnik I	Christ Statue	Christ Statue	Mt. Rushmore

Some of the places listed above failed to capture public interest. Such places that are virtually unknown today include the nuclear plants (Calder Hall), hydro-electric plants (Snowy River), and radio telescopes (Jodrell Bank). One list even included *Sputnik I,* which does not qualify as a specific location.

Expert opinion helps resolve disagreements. During the 1950s the American Society of Civil Engineers (ASCE) selected seven modern (technological) wonders. Their choices included the largest bridge, dam, and skyscraper of the time. In 1995 ASCE gathered a worldwide panel of engineers to select the century's greatest engineering feats that were also of lasting value.

ASCE (1950s)	ASCE (1995)
Panama Canal, Panama	Panama Canal, Panama
Empire State Building, USA	Empire State Building, USA
Transbay Bridge, USA	Golden Gate Bridge, USA
Grand Coulee Dam, USA	Itaipu Dam, Brazil-Paraguay
Hoover Dam, USA	CN Tower, Canada
Colorado River Aqueduct, USA	Eurotunnel, UK-France
Chicago Sewer System, USA	Dutch Dikes, Netherlands

The 1950 list should not have included two dams (which detracts from uniqueness) and a sewer system (which lacks beauty). In contrast, the international panel of 1995 did an excellent job. Their list sets an authoritative standard for engineering feats of the century. They also mentioned in a separate list seven future wonders under construction at that time.

On the other hand, the engineers focused on feats of engineering and did not always consider criteria such as unsurpassed records. For instance, neither the Golden Gate Bridge nor the Empire State Building held the world record in their categories in 1995. The engineers probably accepted these as classic examples of suspension bridges and tall buildings, but neither satisfies the criteria in the introduction to this book. The Akashi-Kaikyo Bridge, just completed in 1998, was listed by the engineers as a future wonder and is so much longer than all other suspension spans that it is unlikely to be surpassed very soon. It should certainly replace the Golden Gate Bridge among the seven wonders of technology. Another future wonder listed by the engineers was Petronas Twin Towers, which has taken the world record for tallest building and bumped the Empire State Building down to sixth tallest. Empire State is not even the tallest building in New York City. Petronas Towers, however, barely surpasses Chicago's Sears Tower, and controversy still surrounds the claim. All are far surpassed by the CN Tower, a skyscraper of a different type. Thus, for this book, we will avoid having two skyscrapers and include the world's tallest monument instead. This monument has the advantage of being unique as well: the Gateway Arch in St. Louis.

Such marvellous feats clearly show man's dominion over the earth. God delegated to man authority over the earth. Man has misused his dominion at times, but at other times he has been a good steward of the earth's resources. Each of the achievements above shows this stewardship. Several of the wonders display man's dominion over obstacles to travel: the Akashi-Kaikyo Bridge and the EuroTunnel conquer large expanses of water, while the Panama Canal overcomes a land barrier. Gateway Arch is a monument to overcoming travel obstacles in America's westward expansion. Others display man's dominion in harnessing powers of nature: Itaipu Dam harnesses water power to provide electricity for cities, and the CN Tower harnesses radio waves for communication. The Dutch Dikes obtain usable space from the sea.

"And God said, Let us make man in our image, after our likeness: and let them have dominion over the fish of the sea, and over the fowl of the air, and over the cattle, and over all the earth, and over every creeping thing that creepeth upon the earth" (Gen. 1:26).

ENGLISH CHANNEL TUNNEL, UK-FRANCE

Matt Webb swam as hard as he could. Night had fallen, and he could not see land. Storms threatened. Large waves blocked his view and choked his breathing with salt sprays. Tiredness spread across his mind and body. His arms ached from twenty hours of swimming, and his thoughts drifted from lack of sleep. He jerked alert at the sight of a shark passing nearby.

Matt Webb had begun his swim August 24, 1875, near Calais, France. He hoped to be the first to swim across the English Channel, but he did not think it would take this long. Lights? Yes, he could see lights in the distance. Success was in sight, and he stayed alert for the last leg. When he finally

Channel Tunnel train

reached land near the white cliffs of Dover, it was August 25, and he had been swimming twenty-one hours and forty-five minutes.

The English Channel stood as a great barrier. It protected England from land attacks and forced her to become a great sea power. Albert Matthieu, a French engineer, first proposed a tunnel in 1802. A tunnel linking France and England would greatly aid land transportation, but both governments rejected all proposals as impractical until 1986.

Work began December 1, 1987. The tunnel structure and machinery form a unique transportation system combining civil, mechanical, and electrical engineering. As a transportation system, the tunnel links the British, French, and Belgian railway systems. There are actually three parallel tunnels, two wide ones and a narrow one, each 131 feet beneath the bottom of the English Channel. The three tunnels are each thirty-one miles long, and twenty-four of those miles pass beneath the sea floor. Although Japan's Seikan Tunnel is a little longer (33.5 miles), only 14.5 miles of the Seikan pass under the sea to link Honshu

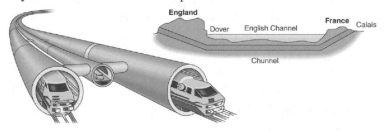

Channel Tunnel entrance

with Hokkaido. Since the English Channel Tunnel is only 2.5 miles shorter but mostly underwater (the world's longest underwater tunnel), it was selected unanimously as a wonder of the world by the international panel of engineers.

Each of the twenty-five-foot-diameter tunnels contains a fourteen-foot-wide train. The 7,600 horsepower engines enable these trains to reach speeds of 87 mph. Each train is half a mile long and can carry 130 cars and buses. Motorists drive their cars right onto the shuttle and remain in their cars for the hourlong ride, which means that most shuttles carry about eight hundred passengers. In addition, the freight shuttle carries up to twenty-eight trucks.

Though underwater and under the sea floor, the train ride is quite comfortable and safe. The twenty-four shuttle carriages, half of which are double-deckers, are brightly lit, soundproof, and even air-conditioned. The smaller 16-foot diameter service tunnel between the large train tunnels provides for maintenance and emergencies. At almost quarter-mile intervals, cross passages eleven feet in diameter connect the service tunnel with the main tunnels. Sliding doors seal off cross passages when they are not in use. Similar steel doors can seal off the main tunnels into equal thirds. Siphons remove rainwater and condensation, and fans circulate air. Three hundred miles of pipes cool the tracks with water, and pistons open and close ducts to relieve pressure that builds up in front of the train. Fiber-optic cables relay information between controllers and engineers.

Inside the Channel Tunnel

Queen Elizabeth II of England and President François
Mitterrand of France presided at the opening dedication on
May 6, 1994. The fifteen thousand workers completed the tunnel in six-and-a half-years, one year behind schedule. Expenses
mounted to 15 billion, twice the amount budgeted, and it also
cost the lives of nine workers.

PANAMA CANAL, PANAMA

The destroyer entered Limon Bay on the Atlantic coast and
headed for Gatún Locks. The captain relaxed as he scanned the
shipyards of Cristóbal, the harbor of Colón, because no enemy
could fire on him during his passage across the neutral canal. A
small boat pulled alongside, and the canal pilot boarded. The
pilot guided the destroyer seven miles along the channel to
Gatún Locks. Small locomotives jockeyed the destroyer into
place with cables so that the back gate could close.

Silently, water filled the lock from below, raising the level of
the ship with it. When the front gate opened, the pilot and locomotives guided the destroyer into the next lock. After yet a third
lock, the ship sailed into Gatún Lake, now eighty-five feet
above sea level. Gatún Dam, which they passed to starboard,
held back the waters of the Chagres River to form Gatún Lake.
At the head of the lake, they entered the eight-mile-long
Gaillard Cut, which permits only one-way traffic. Finally, the
Pedro Miguel Locks and then the Miraflores Locks lowered the
ship to the Bay of Panama. The pilot disembarked after eight
hours of guiding the ship, and the destroyer sailed into the
Pacific Ocean. At that point, the ship had travelled forty miles
between coasts—fifty miles between the open oceans. Although
still quite a distance from battle, the captain resumed his vigil as

they sailed out of the neutral waters toward combat in the Pacific Ocean.

The Atlantic Ocean is east of the Pacific Ocean, right? Yet the battleship entered the Pacific twenty-seven miles east of where it left the Atlantic! Look at the map if you don't believe it.

The wonder of the Panama Canal involves history, medicine, and engineering. Historically, Panama had long been a scene for ocean transits. During the 1849 gold rush, many would-be prospectors sailed to Colón, walked across Panama to Panama City, and then took another boat to California. Profits prompted New York business executives to build a railroad across the isthmus. They finished in 1855 at a cost of $8 million. In 1878 Colombia granted a Frenchman, Lucien Napoleon Bonaparte Wyse, the right to build a canal across its province named Panama. He sold the rights to the constructor of the Suez Canal, Ferdinand Marie de Lesseps. The French also bought the railroad for $20 million. De Lesseps began digging in 1882, but he needed better equipment for digging such vast amounts of dirt.

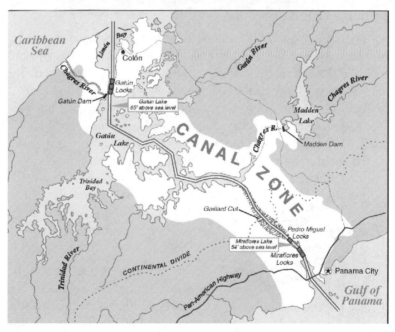

Tropical diseases claimed some twenty-thousand workers, and embezzlement resulted in bankruptcy by 1889. As a result of such setbacks, the company that took over the property wanted to sell the project. Meanwhile, American businessmen went bankrupt trying to build a canal across Nicaragua.

In 1898 the U.S. Navy sent the battleship *Oregon* from San Francisco to Cuba during the Spanish-American War. After the ship sailed over twelve-thousand miles around the tip of South America instead of forty-six hundred miles via a canal, the U.S. Congress recognized that a canal was essential for defense. The United States purchased the French canal rights for $40 million on the condition that Colombia would give the United States permanent use of the canal. The United States offered $10 million plus $240,000 annually after 1913 for the rights, but Colombia wanted more. Panama wanted the benefit of the trade, the French wanted the sale, and the United States wanted the canal. In 1903 Panama, with the help of France and the United States, revolted and declared itself independent. Two weeks later, the new government of Panama accepted the offer. In May 1904, the United States took over the French property.

When the United States undertook this project, the medical problems were at least as great as the historical failures. Disease took the lives of many workers, and the canal region ranked among the most disease-infested areas worldwide. Colonel William C. Gorgas, an American doctor who had wiped out yellow fever in Havana, Cuba, after the Spanish-American War, came to work on the problem. For two years, the only progress on the canal involved disease control. The workers drained swamps and cleared grass and brush where mosquitos swarmed.

By 1906 they had wiped out yellow fever and bubonic plague and decreased the death rate from malaria.

Since the Suez Canal engineers had failed, American engineers knew that building the canal would require no small engineering feat.

Ore and oil carrier
in the Pedro Miguel Locks

In 1907 President
Theodore Roosevelt
assigned the task to
army engineer
George W. Goethals.
With this assignment,
Goethals faced three
challenges. First, he
had to build Gatún
Dam to create the
163-square-mile lake
that would cover half

Gaillard Cut

of the 50-mile passage. Second, he would have to build the six
pairs of locks to raise and lower ships from the oceans to the
lake level. The men built pairs of locks to allow for two-way
traffic. Third, he would have to cut a channel across the hills at
the Continental Divide. This cut, the Culebra Cut, was later re-
named the Gaillard Cut in honor of the engineer who supervised
the work on the channel. The men dug a channel between Gold
Hill and Contractor's Hill and removed 211 million cubic yards
of earth and rock—enough to bury Interstate 90 in dirt ten feet
deep, all the way from Boston to Seattle. This is more than
twice as much as they expected to remove because landslides
kept filling in the dirt that they removed. Some of the dirt aided
construction of the dam. In 1913 there were 43,400 people
working on the canal. The following year, they completed the
canal on time and within the established budget.

Use of the canal has always been heavy. The SS *Ancon* made
the first crossing in August 1914, but a landslide closed the
canal for months in 1915-16. After President Woodrow Wilson
proclaimed the official opening of the canal on July 12, 1920,
many American warships crossed the Panama Canal during
World War II, the Korean War, and the Vietnam War. Currently,
all ships can fit through the 1,000-foot-long and 110-foot-wide
locks except the modern U.S. Navy supercarriers and a few
commercial supertankers. Because of these new ships, plans for
widening the canal or constructing a new sea-level canal with-

Navy ship in the locks

out locks are under investigation. About thirty-four ships pass through the canal daily, and 70 percent of the cargo is headed to or from U.S. ports. Canadian and Japanese cargo accounts for much of the remaining 30 percent.

Costs associated with the canal are phenomenal. Building costs included $40 million to buy the French company, $20 million for sanitation and disease control, $10 million to Panama for property rights, and $310 million in actual construction costs. Due to inflation, the annual payment of $240,000 has increased several times and presently amounts to $20 million besides other fees. The United States makes these payments by charging tolls averaging $32,000 for each ship passing through the canal.

Since the opening of the canal, the United States has controlled it, but this is changing. Originally, the Canal Zone was a U.S. territory like Guam or Puerto Rico. A treaty in 1979 transferred jurisdiction of the Canal Zone to Panama. The business of the canal is still run by an American company, but operation will also transfer to Panama on December 31, 1999. These treaties still permit the United States to use military force to defend the neutrality of this wonder of technology.

From observation platforms near the Miraflores Locks, visitors can see the Panama Canal, which has earned its place among the technological wonders of the world. Though the Suez Canal is twice as long, the builder of the Suez Canal gave up on building the Panama Canal. Length is not the key difficulty in canal building; other factors pose numerous challenges—such as crossing the Continental Divide, linking two oceans, controlling disease, and building large numbers of dams, locks, and channels. These feats make the Panama Canal one of the greatest works of the twentieth century.

ITAIPU DAM, BRAZIL-PARAGUAY

Power courses through water. The media often document fearsome destruction caused by hurricanes, floods, and tidal waves; but even normal seas claim swimmers in their powerful rip tides, shorebreaks, and undertows. White-water rafters and swimmers drown in powerful hydraulics. People build dams to harness this power. In 1956 an earthen dam in Toccoa, Georgia, broke, loosing the waters of Toccoa Creek. This small creek tragically wiped out a college, leaving thirty-nine dead. How much more power is in the Paraná River—a river the size of the Mississippi?

The Paraná River is among the ten largest rivers in the world. At one time, as it flowed across southern Brazil, it roared over Salto das Sete Quedas or Guaíra Falls. These rapids dropped 375 feet to create the most powerful waterfall in the world. At this location, where the town of Guaíra overlooks the river border between Brazil and Paraguay, 470,000 cubic feet of water course down each second. The reservoir from the dam sub-

Spillway at Itaipu Dam

65

merged the falls, but the volume of water still displays the size of the river.

About forty miles downstream, at the point selected for the dam, the river spreads out a quarter-mile wide and two hundred feet deep. In 1978 engineers diverted the river by digging a new channel for the river, 1.25 miles long and almost one-tenth of a mile wide (490 ft.). Changing the course of such a great river required blasting and the moving of fifty million tons of rock and dirt. The next year, when the original riverbed had dried out, they began to build the new dam. Almost five miles long, the dam required enough iron and steel to build 380 Eiffel Towers and enough concrete to build fifteen Eurotunnels.

At last, on October 13, 1982, the dam was completed at a cost of $18 billion. The twelve great gates descended in only eight minutes to seal off the new channel. The churning waters built up behind the dam for fourteen days until the waters were 328 feet above the normal water level. When water began to flow over the quarter-mile-wide spillway, the backed-up waters had already created a new lake covering 520 square miles—more than Lake Champlain. While impressive, this expansiveness is not what gives Itaipu Dam its fame since Owen Falls Dam in Uganda holds back a larger reservoir.

Itaipu Dam attains a maximum height of 738 feet. This surpasses Hoover Dam (Arizona-Nevada) by thirteen feet, a dam which held the record for the highest dam in the world in 1936.

Turbine at Itaipu Dam

However, in 1989, Rogun Dam in Tajikistan took the record from Itaipu Dam, with its 1,099-foot height. Thus, Itaipu's impressive height is not what makes it famous either. Itaipu Dam's claim to fame is its power.

Each second, 160 tons of water pours down a thirty-five-foot-wide tube onto a turbine. This operates a fifty-three-foot-wide generator. If the size of this engine were not enough, the dam has eighteen of these, all working at once. The twelve

Inside Itaipu Dam

thousand megawatts produced could supply energy for the entire states of New York and New Jersey. Itaipu Binacional, a two-nation company, owns the dam. Brazil and Paraguay split the power, but Paraguay uses only one-third of its share and sells the rest to Brazil at a reasonable rate. Not far downstream from the dam, the mighty Paraná River flows into Argentina, and all three countries plan smaller dams to harness this resource and save the costs of imported oil. Itaipu Dam supplies more hydroelectric power than any other dam in the world.

The dam generating the most power in 1942 was Grand Coulee Dam in Washington. Ranked as one of the seven wonders of the world in the 1960s, no dam surpassed its power until Itaipu Dam. For comparison, Grand Coulee Dam is about one mile long across the Columbia River and 550 feet high, required twelve million cubic yards of concrete, and produces 6,500 megawatts of electricity annually with its twenty-seven generators. Itaipu Dam is about five miles long and 738 feet high, and its eighteen generators produce 12,600 megawatts of electricity annually. This is enough electricity to power most of California. If Grand Coulee Dam once belonged among the wonders, then Itaipu Dam belongs in the list and has no rival today.

The town of Foz do Iguaçu, twelve miles south of the dam, marks the mouth of the Iguaçu River where it enters the Paraná River. Since both rivers form international boundaries, three nations meet at this point. Bridges from Brazil cross the Paraná into Paraguay and the Iguaçu into Argentina. The town, therefore, provides a perfect base point for touring Itaipu Dam, its reservoir, and Iguaçu Falls. Flights arrive from major cities of all three nations: Rio de Janeiro, Brazil; Asuncíon, Paraguay; and Buenos Aires, Argentina. Buses run from two major Brazilian cities, but it is a long trip: 650 miles from São Paulo or 930 miles from Rio de Janeiro. The dam and reservoir receive about seven hundred thousand visitors annually.

DUTCH DIKES, NETHERLANDS

Nazi bombers roared overhead and rained bombs on Rotterdam. The bombing killed hundreds of civilians, left seventy-eight thousand homeless, and destroyed twenty thousand houses. Bombs leveled the downtown district of Rotterdam, one of the largest cities in Holland (now called the Netherlands). The Nazi attack of May 14, 1940, destroyed six hundred years of architecture and culture.

Although the Dutch army was forced to surrender, the Dutch spirit still fought on. Most of the Dutch fleet escaped and helped the Allies. Many civilians risked their lives to provide hiding places for Jews.

The Dutch also suffered the flooding of their land for the war effort. After the Allied troops invaded Normandy in June 1944, they wanted to advance from France to Antwerp in Holland. In September, Allied aircraft began bombing dikes at Veere, Vlissingen, Rammekens, and West Kapelle. By October, the weakened dikes gave way. Water poured through the breaches and flooded out the Nazis. It took until February 1946 for the Dutch to repair all their dikes.

The floods during World War II were neither the first nor the last. The Netherlands is one of the Low Countries, and its low elevation makes it an easy target for storms from the North Sea. Around A.D. 1000, the people built the first canals and dikes to help control flooding. They cut trenches to the sea to provide drainage from swamps and shallow lakes, and they also mounded earth into huge ridges as flood barricades called dikes. As small bodies of water drained, land became available for livestock to graze and eventually for farming.

The Dutch people fought the sea for centuries by building dikes. South of Rotterdam, in the province called Zeeland, the Schelde, Maas (Meuse), and Rhine Rivers form a river delta. In 1421, the St. Elisabeth flood destroyed seventy-two villages and claimed ten thousand lives in this region. On February 1, 1953, only seven years after the repairs from the flooding of World War II, a hurricane breached the dikes at sixty-seven different places. Flood waters covered four hundred thousand acres in

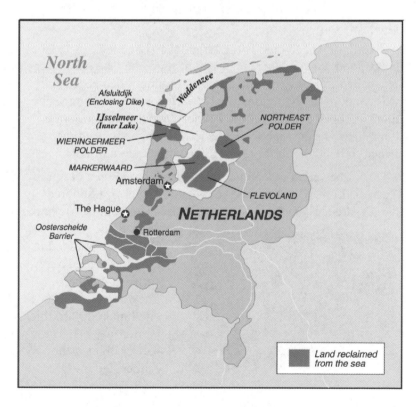

Zeeland and took the lives of eighteen hundred people and twenty thousand livestock. By August, the Dutch had plugged the worst breaks, but it was November before the last dikes were fixed.

Amsterdam is about forty-five miles north of Rotterdam. Huge sand dunes give this region the best natural barrier for protection against the sea. In spite of the dunes' protection, much of this land still runs the risk of flooding because it lies below sea level. The Prins Alexander Polder, which is the lowest point in the country (twenty-two feet below sea level), is one of many polders built since the 1300s. By building a circular dike and pumping out the water, new land is obtained. Originally, windmills supplied the energy for pumping out water, but now electric motors do the work. Because rains can flood a polder, pumps must run continuously to keep the polder empty. Over one-third of all of the land in the Netherlands today lies in polders.

North of Amsterdam is the large lake IJsselmeer. In 1916 a great flood wrecked this area. At that time, the lake was a large bay called Zuider Zee, which means Southern Sea because it was south of the North Sea. In 1667 Hendrik Stevin suggested blocking off the mouth of the Zuider Zee with a twenty-mile-long dike. The damage from the 1916 flood convinced the Dutch to build the Afsluitdijk (Enclosing Dike) after all.

Work began on this great dike in 1927 based on a design by Cornelis Lely, who died two years later. Using five hundred barges, dredges, and floating cranes, the Dutch built two parallel

Afsluitdijk

dams made of clay. Next, they pumped in sand to fill the space between the dams. They completed the one-hundred-yard thick barrier in 1932. The barrier divided the Zuider Zee into the

Waddenzee (Outer or Open Sea) and the IJsselmeer (Inner Sea). Twenty-five discharge sluices control the level of the lake. Partial draining over the next forty years exposed four large new polders—an addition of half a million acres of fertile land— which were sorely needed by the small and densely populated country of the Netherlands. As

Bridge over the Oosterschelde

rivers brought fresh water into the lake and the sluices emptied extra water into the sea, the lake gradually converted to fresh water. In 1976, a four-lane road across the dike was completed.

Work began on an even bigger dike in Zeeland in 1958 to prevent a repeat of the 1953 flood. However, conservationists complained about losing another estuary environment, which was an important stop on the migration route of European birds. The Dutch agreed. Though it was nice to have a large fresh-water lake in the north of Holland, it was also beneficial to have the natural marine estuaries essential to the commercial fisheries in the south. Freshwater lakes could not support the oysters, mussels, and other seafood. Only a great engineering feat could save the estuary and at the same time prevent flooding. In 1976 the Delta Project changed its plans from a dike across the mouth of the estuary to a storm surge barrier. The barrier, or Oosterscheldekering, would permit 85 percent of normal tides to pass through but could be sealed off during storms to prevent flooding. To erect this storm surge barrier, a fleet of specialized ships and another ten years would be needed.

Long poles from the vessel *Mytilus* plunged into the loose sand of the ocean floor. By vibrating the poles, the sands shifted into more compact space. With the seabed compacted, the vessel *Cardium* rolled out two layers of mattresses like long layers of carpet. The sixty-five mattresses forming the bottom layer, each filled with sand, weighed fifty-five-hundred tons. The slightly smaller mattresses of the top layer, each filled with gravel, completed the seabed stabilization phase. Next, the mooring pontoon *Macoma* guided the vessel *Ostrea* into position, and then *Ostrea* lowered each thirteen thousand-ton pier onto its mats. Once in place, the sixty-five piers were filled with sand to increase their weight to over eighteen thousand tons each. One of the largest floating cranes in the world, *Taklift 4*, fitted huge beams across the piers and lowered the gates into place between the piers. The beams contain the highway bridge for cars as well as electrical equipment for operating the gates. Finally, another specialized pontoon, the *Trias,* lowered a bulwark into position behind the piers for extra support. The bulwark is comprised of five million tons of boulders imported from Sweden, Finland, Germany, and Belgium.

Other challenges awaited. Two islands of 150 acres each were created in the sea as construction sites. Three piers at a time could be assembled on each island, and each pier took a year to build. The islands resembled triple polders because each compartment was ten feet below sea level and surrounded by a protective barrier. When a pier was completed, its compartment was flooded so that the *Ostrea* could tow it away. Furthermore, temporary bridges costing $28 million provided access to the

work islands. Also, as with the Golden Gate Bridge, divers inspecting the foundations were limited to ten minutes of calm water between the dangerous tides. One of the islands, Neeltje Jans, houses

Oosterschelde barrier

the gate control station including power and computer-operated controls.

The project was finally completed on October 4, 1986. Queen Beatrix of the Netherlands presided at the dedication. The gates are tested monthly but are needed only during the worst storm or two of the year. The barrier successfully withstood a 1990 hurricane that caused heavy damage in Belgium and England.

Today visitors can visit both the twenty-mile-long Afsluitdijk and the incredible storm surge barrier of the Delta Project. Flights to the Netherlands land at Skiphol, Amsterdam's international airport. On the forty-mile drive north to the Afsluitdikj, visitors can stop and learn about the social aspects, technology, history, and agriculture of the polders at the New Land Information Center at Lelystad or the Zuider Zee Museum at Enkhuisen. Then they can drive across the Afsluitdijk from Den Oever to Harlingen. The road is at the base of the dike on the lake side, but tourists can view both sides at two good observation points: Breezanddijk near Harlingen and Monument Tower, where the last connection sealed off the lake on May 23, 1932.

To visit the Delta Project and the Oosterschelde Barrier, visitors travel forty miles southwest from Rotterdam to Middleburg in the province of Zeeland. The bridge across the Oosterschelde from Veere to Westenschouwen provides distant views of the barrier, but the Delta Expo Center is on the man-made control island Neeltje Jans. Here visitors see the barrier close up and hear audio-visual presentations in several languages, including English. In spring and summer, fifty-minute cruises leave the Expo Center to provide visitors with an opportunity to see the barrier by boat.

CN TOWER, TORONTO, ON, CANADA

Zeke's ears popped, and he felt glued to the floor by the pressure of high-speed acceleration. Is this an airplane? No, he was in an elevator, but at twenty feet per second it felt like a jet taking off. As the elevator climbed, the view through the elevator window even looked like a takeoff. When the elevator reached the top, he stepped off the elevator and looked down at sidewalks 1,150 feet below. He could barely see people and cars; they looked like dots almost a quarter of a mile straight down. His family sat down in the restaurant.

As he ate, Zeke's view changed from the city to Lake Ontario. His father explained that the restaurant revolves slowly so that all diners get a panoramic view. He also explained that tall buildings sway a little like tall trees so the wind will not blow them down. He reassured Zeke that the tower could withstand winds of 260 miles per hour. After supper, they went to the Space Deck and enjoyed the beautiful one-hundred-mile view from 1,470 feet. Zeke picked out buildings along Toronto's skyline, and his father pointed out Buffalo and Niagara Falls in the distance.

After playing miniature golf on one level of the building,

Zeke noticed some people playing a game on another level. His father said they were playing Q-Zar, or laser tag. "Can we play?" Zeke asked. Zeke really enjoyed the game of Q-Zar, and he shot his laser at everyone. Before sunset, they returned to the Space Deck. As the city lights came on, the ocean of lights to the north contrasted with the black void of Lake Ontario to the south. Zeke saw how God had given man dominion over the earth through technology, but the view across the city of millions reminded him of man's need for the gospel. Zeke contemplated his purpose in life as he and his family descended from the highest observation platform in the world.

Zeke was one of 1.7 million visitors who ascended the Space Deck that year. The Skypod, a seven-story structure about two-thirds of the way up the tower, houses the visitors deck and restaurant. The CN Tower reminded Zeke of the Seattle Space Needle, but the CN Tower is exactly three times taller than its little brother in Seattle.

The CN Tower looms 1,815 feet above Toronto, Ontario, in Canada as the tallest skyscraper in the world. A few structures in the world are taller than the CN Tower, but none of them are skyscrapers because they are not freestanding (self-supported) on their own foundations. The highest structures in the world are radio or television antennas supported by guy wires.

Tallest structure (antenna)	height (feet)	date of completion
KVLY-TV, Blanchard, N.D., U.S.A.	2,063	1963
Warszawa, Warsaw, Poland	2,119	1974 (fell 1991)

The Warszawa radio tower was the highest structure ever built, but it collapsed in 1991, leaving the KVLY-TV tower as the highest existing structure. The Bombay TV tower in India, completed in

CN Tower dominates Toronto's skyline.

The CN Tower overlooks the SkyDome.

1998, exceeds the CN tower by approximately twenty-three feet, and three towers in Texas measure 1,977 feet; 1,992 feet; and 2,018 feet respectively. All of these antennas use guy wires, but the CN Tower is self-supported and far surpasses them in beauty as well. The CN Tower is also a classic skyscraper with an observation deck and visitor services. It stands as a testimony to the technology of twentieth-century radio communications.

The CN Tower is a marvel of engineering. Engineers built the top first, and then jacks lifted it eighteen feet per day to insert concrete underneath. Later, they also jacked the SkyPod into place. A Sikorsky helicopter hoisted the antenna to the top. Over fifteen hundred people worked on the building project. They used eighty miles of cable and fifty-three thousand cubic yards of concrete, enough to cover thirty football fields with concrete one foot deep.

Skyscrapers depend on two inventions: safe elevators and steel frames. Without these, buildings were limited to six stories. New York ran the first safe passenger elevator in 1857 at the Haughwout Department Store. In 1875 New York's 260-foot Tribune Building became the tallest building in the world, but with no steel frame it was not a true skyscraper. Ten years later, Chicago became the first to contribute the steel frame. Its ten-story Home Insurance Building of 1885 was partly steel, and its nine-story, 120-foot high Rand McNally Building of 1890 used an all-steel frame. In 1891 Chicago's twenty-story Masonic Temple gained the world record by fourteen feet.

Skyscrapers come in two categories: self-supported towers such as the CN Tower and buildings. Buildings must have mostly inhabited floors used for offices or apartments. The history of the tallest self-supported structure (tower) follows. Notice that the Pharos was destroyed in A.D. 1375, and in the meantime the top block had been removed from the Great Pyramid.

Tallest self-supported structure	year	height (feet)
CN Tower (Toronto, Canada)	1975	1,821
Ostankino Tower (Moscow, Russia)	1971	1,761
Empire State Building (New York, U.S.A.)	1931	1,250
Chrysler Building (New York, U.S.A.)	1930	1,046
Eiffel Tower (Paris, France)	1889	984
Cologne Cathedral (Cologne, Germany)	1880	511
Great Pyramid (Giza, Egypt)	1375	449
Pharos (Alexandria, Egypt)	250 B.C.	560
Great Pyramid (Giza, Egypt)	2600 B.C.	481

New York and Chicago not only invented skyscrapers, but they also perfected them throughout the twentieth century. Not to be outdone by Chicago's Masonic Temple, New York City built ten successive record skyscrapers. The Empire State Building held the record the longest (forty-one years), followed briefly by the two World Trade Center buildings. Chicago reclaimed the skyscraper title and held it for the next twenty-three years with the Sears Tower. Until 1989, New York and Chicago sported all six of the world's highest skyscrapers. These were the only skyscrapers exceeding 1,100 feet.

Building	city	year	height (feet)
Sears Tower	Chicago	1974	1,454
World Trade Tower 1	New York	1972	1,368
World Trade Tower 2	New York	1972	1,362
Empire State Building	New York	1931	1,250
Amoco Building	Chicago	1973	1,136
John Hancock Center	Chicago	1969	1,127

In 1989 Hong Kong joined New York and Chicago with its 1,205-foot Bank of China and the 1,227-foot Central Plaza three years later. However, neither of these structures set a new skyscraper record. In 1997 Malaysia took the world record to Asia with its Petronas Twin Towers.

Tallest building	stories	year	height (feet)	architect
Petronas Towers, Kuala Lumpur	88	1997	1,476	Cesar Pelli
Sears Tower, Chicago	110	1974	1,454	Fazlur R. Khan
World Trade Towers, New York	110	1972	1,368	Minoru Yamasaki
Empire State Building, New York	102	1931	1,250	Shreve, Lamb, Harmon
Chrysler Building, New York	77	1930	1,046	William Van Alen
40 Wall Street, New York	71	1929	927	Severance, Matsui
Woolworth, New York	60	1913	792	Cass Gilbert
Metropolitan Life, New York	50	1909	700	Napoleon LeBrun
Singer Tower, New York	42	1908	612	Ernest Flagg
Park Row Building, New York	29	1899	389	R. H. Robinson
St. Paul Building, New York	16	1899	310	George B. Post
American Surety, New York	21	1895	290	Bruce Price
Masonic Temple, Chicago	22	1891	274	E. C. Shankland
Tribune Building, New York	9	1875	260	Richard M. Hunt

Notice that the Empire State Building was not the first sky-scraper. Ten previous record-setting skyscrapers had been built, and one had even surpassed one thousand feet in height only a year before. Furthermore, the Empire State Building is not the highest building today but has been surpassed by five other buildings (including two sets of twin towers). It is neither the highest in North America, a record that goes to Chicago's Sears Tower, nor even the highest in New York City. The highest buildings of each continent appear below.

Tallest building by continent	stories	year	height (feet)
Petronas Twin Towers, Kuala Lumpur	88	1997	1,476
Sears Tower, Chicago	110	1974	1,454
Commerzbank Tower, Frankfurt	56	1997	981
Rialto Tower, Melbourne	56	1985	794
Carlton Center, Johannesburg	50	1973	722
Parque Central Torre Oficinas, Caracas	56	1990	656

GATEWAY ARCH
ST. LOUIS, MO, USA

Eliel Saarinen read the cable. It was from a man in charge of the 1947 architectural design contest for a monument to be built in St. Louis. Eliel remembered when the man had cabled to inform him that his design had been selected from over two hundred entries as the winning design. Eliel, a well-known architect, had immigrated to the United States in 1923. He had already designed the Helsinki Central Railroad Station in his native Finland and the buildings of the Cranbrook Foundation of Bloomfield Hills, Michigan, where he now served as president of the Academy of Art.

The cable explained that the judges had made a mistake in contacting him. They had confused his name with his son's. They apologized profusely but said that it was actually Eero Saarinen's design that had won the contest. It was quite an embarrassing mix-up for all parties involved.

Eliel felt strange to be upstaged by his son. Yet he was happy that Eero had come into his own. Eliel and Eero had been working as partners since 1938 when they designed the Kleinhans Music Hall in Buffalo. A year later, they would design the General Motors Tech Center in Warren, Michigan. Eliel later designed churches in Columbus, Indiana, and Minneapolis, Minnesota, before his death in 1950.

The bold design of the Gateway Arch won Eero Saarinen a reputation separate from that of his father. Eero's design beautifully symbolized the role of St. Louis as a gateway to the American West. The crossing of the Mississippi River marked the entry of pioneers into the Louisiana Purchase on their way to the Oregon Trail or the California gold rushes. The Louisiana Purchase was the major step of national expansion begun by

Thomas Jefferson. The arch is part of Jefferson National
Expansion Memorial National Historic Site. Today the memorial includes the arch, an underground visitor center and museum, a historic cathedral, and an old courthouse dating from
1839.

In the following year, Eero designed a number of other
buildings, including the Kresge Auditorium and the chapel for
the Massachusetts Institue of Technology (1953); the United
States embassies in Oslo (1959) and London (1960); the John
Deere administrative center in Moline, Illinois; and the Ingalls
Hockey Rink (1959) at Yale University, his alma mater. He de-
signed only one skyscraper—the CBS Building in New York
City. Three other buildings he designed were completed the
year after his death: Bell Labs at Holmdel, New Jersey; the
TWA terminal at Kennedy International Airport; and the Dulles
International Airport.

Eero, who died of a brain tumor in 1961 at the age of fifty-
one, did not even see construction begin on his arch.
Constructed between 1962 and 1965, the arch required 886 tons
of stainless steel. In cross section, the arch consists of equilat-
eral triangles that measure fifty-four feet on each side at the
base but taper to seventeen feet at the top. The base section as
are the largest, each being twelve feet high.

Gateway Arch soars over the St. Louis skyline.

Inside the arch, special
trams climb the legs to observation windows at the top.
Keeping the passengers upright
as they ascend inside the curv-
ing sides of the arch posed an
interesting engineering problem. The answer employed a
design similar to the baskets
on a Ferris wheel. Visitors sit
in small egg-shaped capsules
that hold five people. A train
or tram of eight such capsules

linked together works in each leg of the arch.

When the tram stops near the top after a four-minute ride, visitors climb a short flight of steps to the observation deck, which is sixty-five feet long and seven feet wide and can accommodate one hundred people. The windows offer spectacular views extending thirty miles on a clear day. To the east lies the Mississippi River with its docks and barges and the industrial complex on the Illinois side of the river. The city of St. Louis dominates the view from the other window. The most prominent landmarks of the sprawling metropolitan area on the Missouri side of the river include the old courthouse two blocks due west and Busch Stadium, which is a few more blocks southwest.

The Arch of St. Louis is certainly unique. Many tall monuments are simple obelisks, such as the Washington Monument. At 630 feet high, the arch not only surpasses them in height but also reflects a more challenging construction. While the imposing

Monuments	height (feet)
Gateway Arch (St. Louis, Missouri)	630
San Jacinto Monument (Houston, Texas)	570
Washington Monument (Washington, DC)	555
Great Pyramid (Giza, Egypt)	482
Perry's Victory (Lake Erie, Ohio)	352
Statue of Liberty with base and torch (New York)	302
Soldiers and Sailors Monument (Indianapolis)	284
Motherland (Volgograd, Russia)	270
Liberty Memorial (Kansas City, Missouri)	217
Arc de Triomphe (Paris, France)	164
Bald Knob Cross (Alto Pass, Illinois)	112
largest Egyptian obelisk (Rome, Italy)	105
Stephen A. Douglas Tomb (Chicago, Illinois)	100
Indiana World War Memorial (Indianapolis)	100

heads at Mount Rushmore are sixty feet high, they are too small to make this list.

The first six sections of the arch were lifted into place by a crane. Since the crane could not lift sections higher than seventy-two feet, then special derricks ascended tracks on each leg to raise each successive section into place. The two legs grew until they were only two feet apart. Jacks forced the gap to open to eight feet. When the final section was in place, the jacks were removed, and the legs clamped it into place. The derricks removed the tracks and polished the arch as they descended for the last time.

The shape of the arch is called a catenary curve by engineers and a hyperbolic cosine by mathematicians (it is not a parabola). The most important part is that this shape is the strongest and most stable supporting structure known to man. It is so strong that the bridge sways only eighteen inches in winds of 150 miles per hour.

AKASHI-KAIKYO BRIDGE, JAPAN

January 17, 1995. Earthquake! The Great Hanshin earthquake destroyed the city of Kobe in Japan. The Japanese people experienced all the effects of an earthquake that registered 7.2 on the Richter scale. Some one hundred thousand buildings collapsed and five thousand people died. Others were maimed or trapped under debris. Drivers lost control of vehicles, and Kobe became a disaster area of horrific proportions.

At the time of the quake, the Akashi-Kaikyo Bridge was under construction. Engineers had begun construction in May 1988 using a design that would withstand quakes up to 8.5 on the Richter scale. The Kobe quake center was only 2.5 miles from the bridge, and the previously unknown fault passed right under it. Yet the quake caused no damage except to stretch the bridge an extra 2.6 feet. The amazing technology that withstood such a devastating quake enabled engineers to continue the work after the quake. Within a month, they had compensated for the additional length by redesigning a few girders to make the bridge approaches four feet higher.

The structures that connect the bridge and its cables to the land (anchorages) are the world's largest. The one on the north end of the bridge is the larger of the two. It is 279 feet in diameter and extends 207 feet below the ground. Concrete surrounds the supporting frame, and the anchorage weighs a total of 350,000 tons.

Before the discovery and use of steel, engineers had to place bridge supports close together. The space between the supports is called a *span*. The Alcántara Bridge, an ancient Roman bridge over the Tagus River in Portugal, is 160 feet high and 900 feet long, but each of the two main arches span only ninety-eight feet. Even early modern suspension bridges, such as the 1849 Ohio River Bridge at Wheeling, West Virginia, amazed the world with long spans supported only at the ends.

The Akashi-Kaikyo Bridge now boasts the longest suspension span in the world. The main span between the towers is

History of Record Suspension	year	span (ft.)
Akashi-Kaikyo Bridge, Japan	1998	6,529
Humber Bridge, Hull, England	1981	4,626
Verrazano Narrows Bridge, New York City	1964	4,260
Golden Gate Bridge, San Francisco	1937	4,200
George Washington Bridge, NY-NJ	1931	3,500
Ambassador Bridge, Detroit, USA-Canada	1929	1,850
Benjamin Franklin Bridge, Philadelphia	1926	1,750
Bear Mountain Bridge, New York	1924	1,632
Williamsburg Bridge, New York City	1903	1,600
Brooklyn Bridge, New York City	1883	1,595

Between the towers is a distance of 1.2 miles.

6,529 feet or about a mile and a quarter, making it half as long again as the Golden Gate Bridge. Although there is talk of a longer bridge across the Strait of Gibraltar, the huge span of the Akashi-Kaikyo Bridge is not likely to be surpassed soon.

The Akashi-Kaikyo Bridge has the record span but not the record for total length. Its length between anchorages totals 12,828 feet or about 2.4 miles. For instance, the twin concrete trestle bridge across Lake Pontchartrain in Louisiana is twenty-four miles long. Such long bridges of the trestle or floating pontoon types consist of many short spans. Suspension bridges are notable for their long spans and graceful structure. The five-mile Mackinac Bridge in Michigan is a suspension bridge but uses additional towers to split the length into additional spans.

The designers of the Akashi-Kaikyo were not out to set records. Instead, their goal was to span the strait between the main island (Honshu) and the small island of Awaji, which would form a link to the fourth largest island, Shikoku. Each day between the Inland Sea and Osaka Bay, up to fourteen hundred ships pass through Akashi Strait (*kaikyo* means "strait") . The engineers designed the bridge with towers on the sides of the navigable channel so that the supports would not interfere with shipping.

The towers are the tallest ever built. The towers of the Golden Gate Bridge held the former record at 746 feet high—taller than the Washington Monument, the Arch of St. Louis, or even the Seattle Space Needle. The towers of the Akashi-Kaikyo Bridge surpass the Golden Gate's towers by over 150 feet and must withstand the 180-mile-per-hour winds of Japan's typhoon season. At 928 feet high, the new bridge towers are almost as high as the Eiffel Tower!

In December 1985, the Japanese government decided to build the bridge. The 1986 groundbreaking ceremony was held in April, but actual construction could not begin until the completion of land surveys. By 1987, the surveys had been completed and a test excavation for the towers began.

Construction required ten years, commencing in May 1988 and concluding in April 1998. The construction progressed through six phases. First, huge buckets lowered from barges removed 720,000 cubic yards of silt to expose bedrock. The second phase placed the concrete piers (tower bases). A steel company built huge hollow cylinders 230 feet high and 262 feet across called caissons, and then six tugboats towed each steel caisson across the strait. After being submerged into place, pumps filled the caissons with marine concrete. This process was completed early in 1992, and the resulting structures served as the piers.

During the third phase, cranes built the towers. Each tower consisted of thirty tiers, each of which stood thirty-one feet high. Each tier, in turn, consisted of three parts, or cells, suitable to the 160-ton lifting capacity of the cranes. The cranes climbed each tower to lift each cell into place. Dampers on the seventeenth, eighteenth, and twenty-first tiers of the towers reduce the motion caused by wind. Acting as stabilizers, they dampen both the sway and torsion forces. Each damper consists of a ten-ton pendulum that swings as a counterbalance force.

Suspension cables and cranes during construction

The fourth phase began in November 1993 and involved the stringing of the cables. Helicopters

SEVEN WONDERS
OF THE WORLD

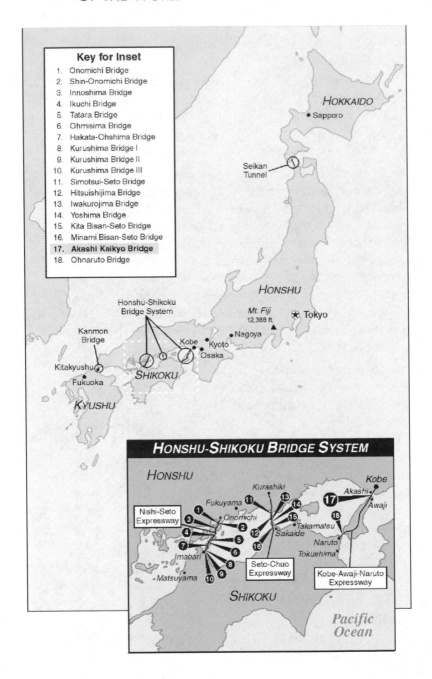

Key for Inset
1. Onomichi Bridge
2. Shin-Onomichi Bridge
3. Innoshima Bridge
4. Ikuchi Bridge
5. Tatara Bridge
6. Ohmisima Bridge
7. Hakata-Ohshima Bridge
8. Kurushima Bridge I
9. Kurushima Bridge II
10. Kurushima Bridge III
11. Simotsui-Seto Bridge
12. Hitsuishijima Bridge
13. Iwakurojima Bridge
14. Yoshima Bridge
15. Kita Bisan-Seto Bridge
16. Minami Bisan-Seto Bridge
17. **Akashi Kaikyo Bridge**
18. Ohnaruto Bridge

HOKKAIDO
• Sapporo

Seikan
Tunnel

HONSHU

Mt. Fiji
12,388 ft. ▲   ☆ Tokyo

Honshu-Shikoku
Bridge System

Kanmon
Bridge   Kobe
                              Kyoto   • Nagoya
Kitakyushu   Osaka
• Fukuoka   SHIKOKU

KYUSHU

HONSHU-SHIKOKU BRIDGE SYSTEM

HONSHU   Kobe
                      Kurashiki   Akashi•
             Fukuyama ⑪   ⑬   ⑰ •Awaji
Nishi-Seto   ①   •Onomichi   ⑭
Expressway ③   ⑮   ⑱
            ④   ②   ⑫ •Takamatsu
            ⑦   ⑤ ⑯ Sakaide   •Naruto
         Imabari   ⑥   Tokushima•
                      ⑧   Seto-Chuo   Kobe-Awaji-Naruto
• Matsuyama ⑩ ⑨   Expressway   Expressway

SHIKOKU

Pacific
Ocean

strung temporary cables between the towers, and then a catwalk was hung from the temporary cables as an aid to stringing the permanent cables. The permanent cables have certain similarities to the cables for a ship's anchor but are far larger. Anchor cables consist of twenty pencil-thin wires braided to form a cable as thick as your wrist. Each bridge cable consists of 290 strands, and each strand consists of 127 wires. This means that each cable contains 36,830 wires (more than the 27,572 used by the Golden Gate Bridge). The complete cable has the thickness of a tree trunk (3.68 feet in diameter), and the 186,000 miles of wire is long enough to encircle the world seven times (nearly twice as much wire as in the Golden Gate Bridge). The cables were completed just before the Great Hanshin earthquake rocked Kobe.

The fifth phase lasted from June to September 1996 as barges, cranes, and carts transported the forty-six-foot-square truss panels into place. The stiffening trusses required more steel than any other part of the bridge. The grand total of 193,200 tons of steel consisted of 89,300 tons for the trusses; 57,700 tons for the cables; and 46,200 tons for the towers. The vast quantity of steel used in the trusses almost doubles the amount of steel used for the giant towers.

The final phase included the paving of the 116-foot-wide roadway and the painting of the bridge. The six-lane road hangs 318 feet above the water, suspended from the cables. The grayish green paint was chosen to harmonize both with the urban environment and with the sea and sky. Both the tower design and the bridge colors were chosen with aesthetic considerations in mind. The greatest success of the 3.3-million dollar project was that no lives were lost during construction.

The Akashi-Kaikyo Bridge opened to traffic on April 5, 1998, as one link in the Kobe-Awaji-Naruto Expressway. The expressway begins in Kobe, and motorists pay a toll to cross the Akashi-Kaikyo Bridge from Tarumi to Awaji. Motorists continue south along the length of Awaji Island and cross the

Ohnaruto Bridge to the town of Naruto on Shikoku. An exhibition center offers books and videos in several languages.

Japan is one of the world's leaders in modern technology and has done an especially remarkable job with bridges and tunnels. The Akashi-Kaikyo Bridge has incorporated several

unique engineering feats besides those of record size. The designers made breakthroughs in aseismic (anti-earthquake) research as well as in wind resistance. The dampers and truss girders were both developed from this research and were tested in special wind tunnels. The aseismic research proved itself during the Great Hanshin quake. Another advancement increased the tensile strength of wires. The engineers used the new, stronger wires to reduce the number of cables from four to two, thus making the entire bridge lighter and reducing the weight on the foundations.

Roads and railroads connect the four main Japanese islands. In 1941, the world's first undersea railroad tunnel linked the largest island, Honshu, to the southern island of Kyushu. In

1958 a double-decker road tunnel also connected the two islands, and the Kanmon Suspension Bridge joined them in 1973. In 1985 the Seikan Tunnel linked Honshu with the northern island of Hokkaido through the longest tunnel in the world. In 1988 the Seto-Ohashi Bridge opened to the southeastern island of Shikoku and set several records. A third expressway is due for completion in 1999. The Honshu-Shikoku Bridge Authority is responsible for constructing, maintaining, managing, and regulating all three expressways between Honshu and Shikoku, including the Akashi-Kaikyo Bridge.

The Seto-Ohashi Bridge set records in its own day and still boasts three of the world's twenty longest suspension bridges. Besides the three suspension bridges, the two-level Seto-Ohashi Bridge incorporates two cable-stayed bridges, a truss bridge, and five viaducts as the Seto-Chuo Expressway leapfrogs across five smaller islands between the towns of Kurashiki and Sakaide. The upper level is a four-lane expressway, and the lower level carries trains such as the Shinkansen Flyers which reach speeds up to 130 mph. The bridge took ten years to build and cost seventeen lives and $9.5 billion.

The third expressway managed by the Honshu-Shikoku Bridge Authority is the Setouchi Shimanami Sea Route or Nishi-Seto Expressway. This route incorporates ten bridges of various types and uses several small islands as stepping stones. It links the town of Nishi near Fukuyama to Kurishima. Two of the suspension bridges rank among the top twenty spans, and two others rank among the ten longest cable-stayed spans worldwide. In fact, upon its completion in 1999, the Tatara Bridge became the longest cable-stayed bridge in the world with a span of 2,920 feet.

Twenty-five longest suspension spans worldwide in 1999			
rank name	country	year	span (feet)
1 Akashi-Kaikyo	Japan	1998	6,529
2 Store Baelt (East Belt)	Denmark	1998	5,328
3 Humber	England	1981	4,626
4 Jiangyin Yangtze	China	1999	4,544
5 Tsing Ma	China	1997	4,518
6 Verrazano Narrows	U.S.A.	1964	4,260
7 Golden Gate	U.S.A.	1937	4,200
8 Hoga Kusten (High Coast)	Sweden	1997	3,969
9 Mackinac	USA	1957	3,800
10 Minami Bisan Seto*	Japan	1988	3,609
11 atih Sultan Mehmet	Turkey	1988	3,576
12 Bosporus	Turkey	1973	3,524
13 George Washington	U.S.A.	1931	3,500
14 Kurishima III**	Japan	1999	3,379
15 Kurishima II**	Japan	1999	3,346
16 Tagus River	Portugal	1966	3,323
17 Forth Road	Scotland	1964	3,300
18 Kita Bisan Seto*	Japan	1988	3,248
19 Severn	England	1966	3,241
20 Shimotsui Seto*	Japan	1988	3,084
21 Xiling Yangtse	China	1996	2,952
22 Ohuaruto	Japan	1988	2,874
23 Tacoma Narrows II	U.S.A.	1950	2,800
24 Oakland Bay	U.S.A.	1936	2.310
25 Bronx-Whitestone	U.S.A.	1939	2,300

*span of the Seto Ohashi Bridge (*Minami* means "south," *Kita* means "middle")
**span of the Nishi-Seto Expressway

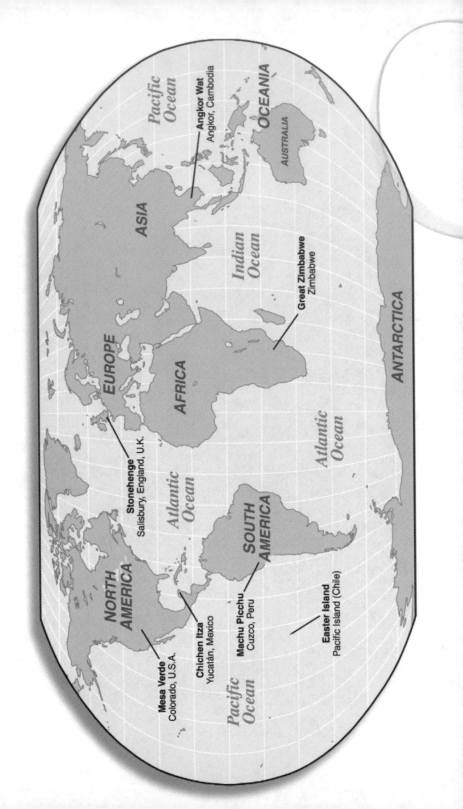

Seven

archaeological

Wonders

7 The Seven Archaeological Wonders

An archaeological wonder of the world is a ruin that reveals the mystery of human civilization. The seven sites selected are undoubtedly the most famous such places worldwide and are popular destinations for tourists. Angkor Wat is sometimes listed as a modern wonder of the world, but it was in ruins when it was rediscovered in the jungles. It is probably the most wondrous of the archaeological wonders, though it is not the most visited. Stonehenge may well be the most famous and most visited, while Mesa Verde, Chichén Itzá, and Machu Picchu display the heritage of the native peoples of the Western Hemisphere. Even Hillman Travel includes Machu Picchu among the Seven Wonders of the World (see p. 131). The mysterious structures of Easter Island and Great Zimbabwe have also captivated human imagination since their discovery. All seven are shown on the map below.

Each of these seven wonders has an air of mystery related to its lack of recorded history. These construction feats accomplished by cultures that have disappeared from the earth are enigmas, sources of human curiosity and speculation. Each left dwellings in inaccessible places, unknown "hieroglyphics," or large temples from unknown religions.

No other ancient sites can compete with these for interest except the Great Pyramid, which need not be covered again. Egypt's Valley of the Kings at Karnak was bypassed by the ancient writers, and the treasures of King Tut have been removed from their original location. The Colosseum of Rome lacks the mystery and intrigue of these vanished civilizations. Indian ruins at Teotihuacan, Copán, Lake Titicaca, and Canyon de Chelly fail to reach the fame of the classic examples of Indian ruins at Mesa Verde, Chichén Itzá, and Machu Picchu.

SEVEN WONDERS
OF THE WORLD

The seven archaeological wonders represent six continents (if Australia is expanded to include all of Oceania). Each of the seven exhibits a culture that preceded modern recorded history. Each civilization arose and flourished in God's sovereignty but perished, having rejected the grace of God. God is patient and merciful, but when the sins of a civilization ripen, God's punishment falls. Notice the evidences of idolatry in each culture as the object of God's wrath, but also notice that God permitted these civilizations to advance to such a degree that their monuments inspire wonder to this day. God in His grace also permits the ruins to remain so that man can learn the result of civilizations that reject Him.

"For all have sinned, and come short of the glory of God" (Rom. 3:23).

"The wicked shall be turned into hell, and all the nations that forget God" (Ps. 9:17).

Stonehenge reconstruction showing central altar slab

STONEHENGE, SALISBURY, ENGLAND, UNITED KINGDOM

"What mean ye by these stones?" (Josh. 4:6) asked children in Israel when they saw twelve huge stones by the Jordan. The older men of Israel explained that they had set up the stones as a monument to the time when God parted the waters and brought Israel across the Jordan River on dry ground.

Another pile of stones stands on the Salisbury Plain ten miles from the train station at Salisbury in the county of Wiltshire, England. No elderly men remain, however, to tell modern children why people erected these stones. *Henge* refers to a collection of stones standing upright or placed as a bridge across standing stones. Thus, the Saxons called this place *Stonehenge*.

The large standing stone slabs, over thirteen feet high and weighing twenty-six tons each, formed a circle, but now some of them have fallen down. Several of the crosspieces or lintels still bridge adjacent slabs. Inside this circle, a horseshoe shape of stones faces northeast. The horseshoe consists of the largest stones—up to twenty-four feet high and weighing up to forty-five tons. A few of the lintels still bridge these huge stones to form *trilithons* (three-stone structures). Just inside the outer circle stand the remains of a circle of small stones, and inside the large horseshoe stand the remains of a horseshoe of small stones.

A circular ditch, three hundred eleven feet across (more than a football field), encloses the whole structure. A circle of fifty-six equally spaced holes, now known as "Aubrey Holes," has been located just inside the ditch. These holes are named after John Aubrey, the man who discovered the site in the seventeenth century. A large "heelstone" stands outside the ditch.

No records remain from the original builders to help man know why this structure was made. Since only God knows the true purpose, speculations abound. In the Middle Ages, people called the place Giant's Dance because they thought that a race of giants had built it. A seventeenth century architect concluded that the ruins belonged to an ancient Roman temple built around A.D. 79 for the god Coelus. In the eighteenth century, William Stukeley popularized the view that Druids had built the place for sacrificial rites.

Modern archaeologists have shown that the ruins date from between 1800 and 1400 B.C. This disproves the above theories. There was no Roman architecture anywhere before the eighth century B.C., and the Druids did not arrive in the British Isles before 700 B.C. In 1963 Professor Hawkins showed that the horseshoe of stones and the heelstone line up with the sunrise at the summer solstice. He showed that the builders could have used the circle of stones as markers for astronomical observations in order to calculate the eclipses and phases of the moon. Although some people think that Stonehenge was used for occult and astrological rites, it could simply have been used for determining when to plant and harvest crops. The Bible says that God created the stars "for signs, and for seasons, and for days, and years" (Gen. 1:14), so studying the heavens is practical for keeping track of years and seasons. Speculations did not cease, though, and in the 1970s Erich Van Danigan claimed that aliens from space had set up the monoliths. His speculations in *Chariots of the Gods* provoked immediate rebuttals, such as *Crash Go the Chariots.*

Several other aspects of Stonehenge are also intriguing and

provoke many more speculations. The builders used a type of stone called bluestone. The closest quarry for bluestone is two hundred miles away in the Prescelly Mountains of

Two upright stones support a lintel to form a trilithon.

Wales. How could people of that era obtain and transport the heavy slabs over such long distances and then erect them? No one knows for sure, but some theorize that the builders used rafts on rivers and rollers on land, and that they raised the huge stones with ropes, levers, and wood scaffolding.

Human remains from cremation were found in the Aubrey Holes, and these suggest to some that Stonehenge was a necropolis, which means "city of the dead." The many barrows or earth mounds piled over burial sites nearby lend support to this graveyard theory.

The British Isles contain other circular stone ruins, including Avebury near Stonehenge, Newgrange in Ireland, and others as far as the Shetland Islands. In fact, similar structures are found near Carnac in France and as far away as the Mediterranean Sea. However, Stonehenge is unquestionably the most famous of them all. Some say it is the pinnacle of achievement of the vanished culture, and its fame is evidenced by replicas in America, the best of which overlooks the Columbia River at Maryhill, Washington. Stonehenge is the most unique archaeological site in northern Europe and may be the most famous archaeological site in the world.

GREAT ZIMBABWE, ZIMBABWE

"Mwali Symbaoe Dzata!" The voice thundered in the temple, yet no speaker could be seen. The tribesmen quaked in fear at the enigmatic statement. No one had ever seen Mwali, their god-king. But his voice thundered daily instructions to them, and he seemed able to see them and know their every move.

The priest knew the tensity of the situation. Cannibals threatened the prosperity of the entire realm. For several years, they had attacked villages on the outskirts of the empire, capturing them one by one and leaving no survivors. Last month, rumors of danger had caused workers to flee from several of the gold mines. With the mines abandoned, the trade with the coast 250 miles away suffered. Furthermore, messengers had brought word just yesterday that cannibals were assembling to attack Symbaoe, the capital itself. The tension caused internal strife: some factions wanted to flee while others wanted to build a stronger defense.

Beside the altar, the priest rose and petitioned for clarification, "Great Mwali, ruler in Symbaoe, shall your people abandon Symbaoe and go to Dzata?" The echoes of his affirmative answer rang loudly through the temple and hid the quavering voice of the dying god-king. Guards watched the road from Fortress Hill while the citizens gathered their valuables and

Conical tower inside the Great Enclosure

herds. Each would also have to transport part of the temple treasures: gold, oriental porcelain, and Persian glass. Could they escape before the cannibals arrived?

The story above dramatizes tribal legends. The BaLemba tribe of South Africa claims descent from the builders of Symbaoe, now called Zimbabwe. Their legends describe their northern homeland ruled by King Mwali who ruled from a stone fortress. Anyone who saw him was condemned to death. People heard his words to the high priest, which echoed loudly, but they never saw him. When he died, one faction migrated to Dzata in South Africa and became the BaLemba tribe.

The ruins at Great Zimbabwe agree with the tribal legends. The huge stone wall, 830 feet in circumference ranged from sixteen to thirty feet high and from as much as sixteen feet thick at

Exterior stonework of the Great Enclosure

the base to as little as eight feet thick at the top. It enclosed various platforms, passages, and rooms. Two stone towers add to the mystery of the Great Enclosure. The higher tower stands thirty feet high but has neither an inside (it is solid rock) nor outside staircase. Since few African builders used stone, preferring mud or wood, the entire construction is uniquely intriguing. In fact, the stonework is excellent. No glue, mortar, or cement was used; instead, stonemasons fitted each brick precisely into place. The fits are so exact that not even a knife blade can be inserted between the bricks.

Similar stonework adorns the rock cliffs rising two hundred feet above the plain of the Great Enclosure. The rocky cliffs include caves and overhangs that have been bricked in to form rooms. The pathway to this Hill Fortress narrows to single file. One of the caves has resonance features similar to a whispering tunnel. A person speaking in the cave is heard loud and clear in the Great Enclosure far below. This explains how the king could remain out of sight and still speak loudly. Besides information obtained from his high priest, he could also spy from the cliffs into the enclosure.

The Shona or Mashona people are still the predominant group in modern Zimbabwe. Their Mwanamutapa Empire apparently stretched across most of the modern nation of Zimbabwe and into adjacent nations of Botswana, South Africa, Mozambique, and Zambia. The Rozwi faction rebelled against the ruling Karanga group and founded their own Changamire Empire in the fifteenth century. Around 1830, the Nguni peoples subjugated most of the Changamire Empire, which left Great Zimbabwe abandoned. The Matabele tribe, which claims descent from the conquerors of the Shonas, say that the Abarozwe, a tribe known as builders, built the Great Enclosure to protect livestock from wild animals. Certainly, there may have been livestock at Great Zimbabwe at various periods, but the evidence of iron and gold smelting proves that an advanced civilization developed here—far beyond the capacities of nomadic shepherds.

The rich gold mines as well as copper and ivory permitted the empire to trade. Delicate china from Nanjing, glazed earthenware from Persia, glass from Arabia, oriental porcelain, and beads from India and Indonesia have all been found in Great

Hill Fortress

Zimbabwe. These artifacts date from A.D 600-1300, but the staggering size of the gold mines suggest that the civilization existed for hundreds of years previously. The Portuguese historian of 1552, João de Barros, located Great Zimbabwe and found that neither Arabs nor Africans could read the inscription over its entrance. This means that by the time of his writing, the ruins were already centuries old—so old that knowledge of the language had been lost.

Mystery, then, surrounds Great Zimbabwe. When was it founded? Why? By what people? No one knows for sure, but theories abound. In the sixteenth century, the Portuguese heard that Sofala, a port on the coast of Mozambique, was the biblical city of Ophir, where King Solomon had obtained his gold (I Kings 10:10-11). Arab records agree that Sofala, the port through which the gold trade passed, was rich in gold. Great Zimbabwe stood in the heart of the gold region. The many foreign goods prove that Great Zimbabwe traded with lands as far away as China and that its gold would have been famous throughout the known world. Sofala and Great Zimbabwe are possible candidates for ancient Ophir, but proof that the city existed before Christ remains elusive.

In 1867 the German explorer Karl Mauch and a hunter Adam Rauch rediscovered the ruins and thought it was the Palace of the Queen of Sheba. In 1906 David Randall MacIver first realized that native Africans had built the city. Archacological digs verified that the structures reflected strictly African styles (except for the imported valuables). A South African journalist, Wilfrid Mallows, thinks that Great Zimbabwe was the central city for the ninth-century slave trade with Arabia.

Historical records also flavor the mysteries. Eratosthenes wrote that the hardy Sabaean mariners had many colonies and were the richest nation in the world. Sabaean ruins in Ethiopia suggest that Great Zimbabwe could have been a Sabaean colony. In fact, a sixth-century Egyptian monk wrote that Sabaeans from Aksum searching for gold journeyed to a region so far south that winter there corresponded with summer in Egypt. On the other hand, old maps show the entire region ruled by King Monomotapa, and Portuguese records also describe invasions of Zimba cannibals into the kingdom of Monomotapa.

Today, from the international airport at Harare, the capital of Zimbabwe, domestic flights and buses travel two hundred miles

to Masvingo. Buses run the last seventeen miles to Great
Zimbabwe. The governing officials of Zimbabwe have adopted
the soapstone bird sculptures found among the ruins of Hill
Fortress as a national emblem. The country of Zimbabwe is
proud to trace its heritage to this wonder of the world—the only
known ancient metal-working civilization south of the equator.

MESA VERDE, COLORADO, USA

"Where did that cow get off to," asked Richard Wetherill.
The snow whipped at their faces. "Hope he didn't fall off that
cliff," said Charlie Mason. They approached the cliff and looked
across the canyon through the swirling snows. "Look at that!
It's a cliff palace!" The riders reigned in their horses and gazed
at a city of ancient Indian dwellings nestled in the steep cliffs
across the canyon. The two cowboys temporarily forgot their
stray cow and took a side trip around the edge of the canyon toward the cliff dwellings. At length, they scrambled down to the
spacious alcove—larger than a football field—containing the cliff
palace. They collected a few souvenirs as they wandered among
the ruins. Later, at home, they showed their prizes to their
friends and told them about Cliff Palace. The name stuck.

The discovery of Cliff Palace on December 18, 1888, led to
visits by later explorers and tourists. In the Southwest and
California, many places have Spanish names. Plateaus are often
called *mesas*, and Cliff Palace hides in the cliffs on the side of
Mesa Verde, or Green Mesa. In 1906 the area became Mesa
Verde National Park. Park workers have replaced fallen bricks
to help visitors enjoy the ruins, but no theoretical reconstruc-
tions of roofs have been added. Cliff Palace has 217 rooms plus
twenty special ceremonial rooms called *kivas*.

Kivas are circular pits, with a shelf or bench along the inside wall. The bench is interrupted by six pillars to support a wooden roof. Indians entered by descending a ladder through the roof, and smoke from the central fire

Reconstructed kiva showing the ladder through the roof as the entrance

pit escaped through the same opening. Fresh air entered a ventilation shaft from the surface and replaced escaping smoke and air. A brick heat deflector directed heat throughout the room. Across the fire pit from the deflector, there was a small shallow hole, called a *sipapu,* or spirit hole.

Modern archaeologists call the builders of Cliff Palace the *Anasazi,* a term used by the modern Navajo Indians for the builders, meaning "ancient ones." Cliff Palace proves that the Anasazi were good builders. They built with stones, neatly arranged in rows and cemented with clay. They covered their buildings with a pinkish-white plaster, and they painted decorations on the interior walls. The exterior plaster peeled off long ago, but a few of the interior paintings can still be seen. The large number of rooms shows that Cliff Palace could have housed four hundred people. Some buildings rise up to four stories high. The Anasazi cut small indentations into the cliff for handholds and toeholds in climbing and descending the cliffs as they brought supplies from their fields on the mesa. They made pottery, cloth, and baskets. They grew corn, squash, and beans,

and they raised turkey for meat and feathers. They carried water up the precarious cliffs from nearby springs.

Modern Hopi Indians claim descent from the cliff

Cliff Palace contains more than a dozen circular kivas

dwellers of Mesa Verde. The Hopi migrated south and now live in pueblos, villages of adobe (sunbaked clay bricks). They still use kivas for social gatherings, religious ceremonies, and workrooms. The Hopi say that the sipapu is the entrance to the underworld. Looms and sipapus found at Mesa Verde prove that Anasazi used kivas in the same ways as the Hopi. This gives some support to the accuracy of their ancestral claims.

Why would Indians live in cliff dwellings and face the daily challenges of entering and leaving? Once there, why would they leave? No one knows for sure, but many have theories. One likely possibility is that the cliffs served as forts, easily defended from raids by neighboring tribes or neighboring villages within the tribe. For dwellings without inside water sources, the residents brought water from springs and stored it in large pottery vessels. There was no need to withstand very long sieges because they could pelt the enemies with stones or shoot arrows. Enemies would also have to leave for supplies. For defense against raids, cliff dwellings were ideal. The agricultural peoples of China solved the problems of nomadic raids with the herculean task of building the Great Wall. The Indians solved the same problem more easily by moving their homes, but the solution required a lifestyle of strength and agility. Perhaps drought caused them to leave for greener pastures after they had depleted the mesa soils.

Remains from the trash heap and burial sites below the cliffs

show that the Indian men grew to be about five feet five inches tall, or about the same height as European men in that period. Women were about three inches shorter. The

Square Tower House

Indians lived about thirty-three years, but only half of the children lived beyond age five. They inhabited Cliff Palace for about one hundred years. Apparently, they lived on top of the mesa, first in the pit houses from A.D 500-750 and then in pueblo structures made of stone from 750-1300. Tree ring dating from the beams of the roofs suggest that they lived in the cliff dwellings during their last one hundred years in the area (after A.D 1200).

Today, visitors can drive to Mesa Verde National Park in the southwest corner of Colorado or fly to nearby Durango and take a bus to the park. Tours of Cliff Palace are the highlight for most visitors. However, there are hundreds of ruins in Mesa Verde National Park, including pit houses, pueblos, and cliff dwellings. Far View House and Sun Temple are the more famous pueblo style ruins that visitors can explore on their own. Of the many other cliff dwellings, some such as Square Tower House, must be viewed from observation points. The four-story Square Tower House is the tallest ruin in the park. Visitors can explore Spruce Tree House, where a self-guided tour leads to a restored kiva that can be entered by a ladder through the roof. Balcony House requires a guided tour due to the popularity of the tunnel and ladders on the route. Two other cliff dwellings open to the public are on Wetherill Mesa.

American Indian ruins include the Incan ruins of South America, the Maya and Aztec ruins of Mexico, and the many Indian mounds of the eastern United States (some are animal-shaped). Besides Mesa Verde in Colorado, there are also cliff dwellings in three other states. The national monuments with cliff dwellings are as follows: Canyon de Chelly, Walnut

Canyon, Navajo, and Tonto in Arizona; Bandelier, Gila Cliff
Dwellings, and Puye Cliff Dwellings in New Mexico.
Canyonlands National Park in Utah also has some cliff
dwellings.

Mesa Verde, however, is unique. Chichén Itzá in Mexico and
some of the burial mounds (the largest mound is at Cahokia
Mounds near East St. Louis, Illinois, and is one hundred feet
high) are larger, but the size of Cliff Palace is equally impressive when one remembers that all building materials were carried up the cliffs using the small footholds and handholds. Cliff
Palace is not as tall as the five-story cliff dwelling at
Montezuma's Castle, south of Flagstaff, Arizona; but Cliff
Palace had the most rooms, supported the largest population,
and covered the most area of any cliff dwelling. Mesa Verde
also provides the widest variety of Indian dwellings (pit, pueblo,
and cliff) that include rock paintings. These relics contribute to
the mystery surrounding the short occupancy of the cliff
dwellings. The scenic, yet rugged, setting captures our imagina-
tions regarding the lifestyle of the Indians. These various facts
make Mesa Verde the most famous and most visited Indian
ruins in the world.

CHICHÉN ITZÁ,
YUCATAN, MEXICO

David Kelley sounded out the symbols on the ancient stone
building, "Kakupakal." It stunned him; the translation really
worked! Kelley knew that records from the Spanish colonial era
stated that Kakupakal, meaning "Fiery Serpent," had been the
name of a great Maya leader and the founder of an important

city. Now he had found that leader's name inscribed at a Maya city, Chichén Itzá.

El Castillo

Kelley had read the old works about Mayan inscriptions, but this new work of Yuri Knorosov in 1952 had broken the code for the first time. Kelley reviewed the history. When Cortés conquered the Aztecs at Tenochtitlán in 1521, priests accompanied the conquistadors in order to convert the Indians. Soon after, when conquistador Francisco de Montejo came to Mexico's Yucatán Peninsula, Diego de Landa, a Franciscan priest, obtained what he thought was the Mayan alphabet from one of the few Aztecs who could still read the ancient writings. By 1800, both Mexicans and Europeans had lost all knowledge of reading Mayan. After 1832, Constantine Rafinesque and others began deciphering the Maya calendar and dates, but when they used de Landa's alphabet to read words, they found only nonsense. Kelley had recently read the work of Yuri Knorosov, a communist scholar in the Soviet Union. While ignoring all the communist propaganda in the work, Kelley recognized that Yuri Knorosov had corrected de Landa's error. Mayan was written, not with letter symbols but with syllable symbols. Kelley's discovery of the Maya leader's name had just proved that Knosorov's translation method was correct.

Kelley walked past the Temple of the Warriors and its rows of pillars decorated with eagles, jaguars, and Toltec warriors. Apparently, the Toltec Indians of Central Mexico had traded with or perhaps conquered the Mayas of Chichén Itzá at one time. This also explained the similarity of their main gods, which Mayas called Kukulcan and Toltecs called Quetzalcoatl.

Kelley climbed the north stairs of the nine-tiered pyramid now called the *El Castillo* (meaning "castle"). The seventy-five-foot-high pyramid had four sides perfectly aligned with the compass points. The staircase on each side split the nine tiers into eighteen halves, one for each Maya month. Each of the four staircases had ninety-one steps, which together with the top platform totalled the 365 days of the Maya year. Artistic panels surrounded the tiers, one for each of the fifty-two years in the Maya cycle (like a century). Kelley entered the pyramid through a passage on the north side, where narrow steps led to two small chambers. One chamber had an idol of Chac Mool, a god carved in a reclining position with his knees and head up and an altar on his belly. As Kelley entered the other chamber, a huge red jaguar looked at him through eyes of green jade. In the gloom, it looked eerie, though he knew that it was just an ornate throne.

While admiring the architectural beauty, Kelley cringed at the evidence of bloody pagan rituals. At the seventy-five-foot-deep Well of Sacrifice, he reflected on the fact that skeletons found show that living persons, many of them children, had been thrown into the well to appease the rain gods during famines.

The walls of the Maya ball court stood ninety feet apart, rising twenty-seven feet high and extending for 272 feet, almost as long as a football field. The ball court was the largest in Central America. The artwork on the sides of the court showed that players had to get a ball through rings at the ends of the court without using their hands, similar to soccer. The artwork also proved that the games involved a life and death struggle—decapitation for the losers.

Ballcourt at Chichén Itzá

Nearby, stood the most gruesome structures: the Platform of the Jaguars, Skull Rack, and the Platform of the Eagles. Carvings at these platforms showed rows of human skulls on stakes and eagles ripping out human hearts. Kelley knew that these carvings reflected Maya rituals to placate the gods. In some artwork, the heads of victims were raised on stakes or the still-throbbing hearts of others were sacrificed on their bloody altars. Another temple depicted Kukulcan with a human heart in its mouth.

Observatory at Chichén Itzá

Through his research, Kelley learned where all the inscriptions were among the ruins of over one hundred structures at Chichén Itzá. The thirty restored buildings included smaller ball courts and temples in addition to the famous ruins explained above. Another group of ruins stood nearby to the south. The small pyramidal tomb of the high priest had an observatory, a cave, and a well for drinking water. Ornate carvings adorned two ruins named by the Spanish: the Nunnery with its animals and flowers and the Church with its beak-nosed rain god, Chac. A fifteen-minute walk farther south through the jungle and mosquitos led to a third set of ruins, the unrestored ruins of Old Chichén. Three miles east, Balancaché Cave had cave formations, a lake with blind fish, and artifacts carved with the Toltec rain god, Tláloc.

Maya civilization in Mexico, Belize, Guatemala, Honduras, and El Salvador traces back to about 1000 B.C. The linguistic breakthroughs have made much Mayan readable, but the language is not fully deciphered even today. Chichén Itzá seems to date from about A.D 435, but the oldest known specific Maya date translates into A.D 879, which suggests that the city reached its peak even later. About 1224, another city, Mayapan, conquered Chichén Itzá and caused its decline. Perhaps the idolatry and cruelty explain its decline. God is patient, but He eventually destroys the cruel as He did when He destroyed the Assyrians for their cruelty (Isa. 14:25).

Tourists from all over the world flock to Chichén Itzá, the most famous Maya ruin, in the state of Yucatán, Mexico. Every evening, popular multimedia sound and light shows are presented in English and Spanish. The most popular times to visit are on the spring and fall equinoxes. The Mayas built the pyramid so that shadows cast by the north terrace look like a snake. The shadow aligns with a sculpture of a serpent's head to complete the illusion.

In order to visit these Maya ruins, tourists can fly to Mérida or Cancún. Mérida is seventy-five miles from the ruins and Cancún is 125 miles away, but tours can be arranged. Trains and buses pass the ruins on the one-hundred-mile journey from Mérida to Valladolid.

Chichén Itzá is the classic central American Indian ruin. It displays all the typical structures from pyramids and temples to ball courts. Its observatories, Well of Sacrifice, and nearby caves add to its mystique. It also displays the fine masonry and precise astronomical alignments known in Maya and Toltec ruins, culminating in the fabulous serpent illusion. While the Toltec pyramid at Teotihuacán is larger (and among the largest in the world), it is the calendars and inscriptions of Chichén Itzá that held the key to the secrets of these civilizations. It still retains some of those intriguing secrets as a wonder of the world.

EASTER ISLAND
PACIFIC ISLAND, CHILE

"Impossible," said the university professor. "Ancient Polynesians had no boats." Thor Heyerdahl countered, "They had balsa wood rafts." The professor laughed, "So you expect me to believe that Indians rafted across the Pacific Ocean!"

Long-eared statues of Easter Island

Heyerdahl believed he could prove that the first Polynesians were South American Indians. In Peru, the Indians tell legends of their Inca ancestors driving out the tribe that built Tiahuanaco on Lake Titicaca. The conquered people had been led by Kon-Tiki, the sun king. Modern Polynesians in Fatu Hiva say that Tiki, the son of the sun, led their ancestors from a land of mountains to the east. Also, the Polynesian pyramid and statue styles reflect those of Lake Titicaca. Sweet potatoes, known to have originated in the New World, are found throughout Polynesia. Still, nothing would convince the skeptics. Heyerdahl felt disgusted.

Heyerdahl gazed intently at a bearded face on a four-sided red column that stood at Tiahuanaco, the pre-Inca ruins near the shores of Lake Titicaca in the Andes of Bolivia. Heyerdahl carefully copied the face of Kon-Tiki onto the square sail of his raft. He had copied his balsa wood raft design from the ancient Indians' designs. Thor set sail on his raft, *Kon-Tiki,* with five friends on April 28, 1947. On August 7, after more than three months, they ran aground at Raroia in the middle of Polynesia. They had sailed forty-three hundred miles across the Pacific Ocean.

The scholars still scoffed: just because an Indian craft could cross the ocean did not prove that any actually did. They believed that Asians first discovered and peopled Polynesia, starting about A.D. 500. Easter Island, the most easterly of all Polynesian islands, would have been the last inhabited—about 1300 at the earliest. Its brief history made excavation useless.

Easter Island held a key to checking his theory. If Polynesia was actually settled from the east as Heyerdahl believed, Easter

Island would have been the first settled. He eagerly studied its history. Jacob Roggeveen, a Dutchman, named the small island (only forty-five square miles) when he landed there on Easter Sunday in 1722. He saw giant stone heads standing in rows along the banks facing inland. The long-eared heads had red stones for hair, much like some of the natives who had lengthened their earlobes and tied their red hair in topknots.

The first communication with the islanders came in 1774, when Captain Cook's Hawaiian sailor found their Polynesian language similar to his own. The natives claimed to have descended from the statue makers called the Long Ears, who had come to the island twenty-two generations ago (or about 550 years ago) from the east. The natives also told Captain Cook that the Short Ears had come later from the west and had caused wars, ending the statue making. The natives called their island *Rapa Nui,* but in all their legends they referred to it as *Te Pito o te Henua,* or the "Navel of the World." This name came because of its isolation—so far from other land that it has been called the most isolated island in the world. The natives knew more stars than places because the moon seemed closer than the invisible lands. They described their island as "east of the sun and west of the moon."

Heyerdahl arrived on Easter Island and looked around. He visited many of the more than six hundred stone heads (called *moai*) scattered around Easter Island. Most of the giant heads were ten to twenty feet high, but the largest finished head was thirty-two feet high and weighed one hundred tons. Later, he

found an unfinished head over sixty-six feet high and weighing three hundred tons. The stone for the heads was quarried from the nearby volcanic crater Rano

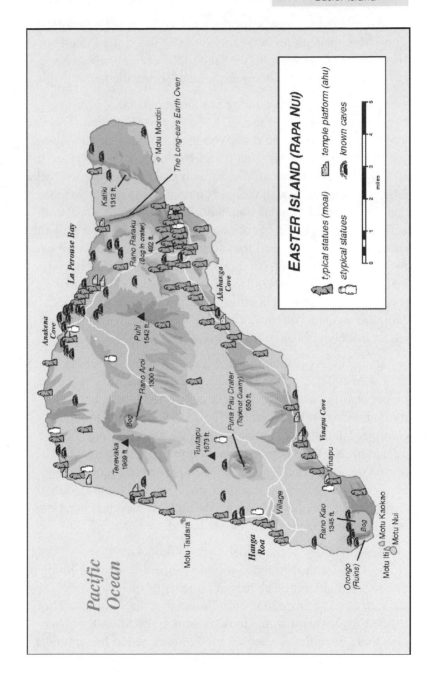

EASTER ISLAND (RAPA NUI)

typical statues (moai)
atypical statues
temple platform (ahu)
known caves

miles
0 1 2 3 4 5

Pacific
Ocean

Motu Moratiri
The Long-ears Earth Oven
Katiki
1312 ft.
La Perouse Bay
Rano Raraku
(Bog in crater)
492 ft.
Akahanga
Cove
Anakena
Cove
Puhi
1542 ft.
Rano Aroi
1300 ft.
Bog
Terevaka
1969 ft.
Tuutapu
1673 ft.
Puna Pau Crater
(Topknot Quarry)
650 ft.
Vinapu Cove
Vinapu
Motu Tautara
Village
Rano Kao
1345 ft.
Hanga
Roa
Bog
Motu Iti
Motu Kaokao
Motu Nui
Orongo
(Ruins)

Raraku, but the red stones for the six-foot diameter topknots came from quarries on the outer slopes of the crater Puna Pau. He found reeds growing in the lake in the crater of Rano Kao, caves everywhere, and many stone platforms called *ahus*.

Heyerdahl's team began excavating at Vinapu, where the largest ahu stood fifteen feet high with a three-hundred-foot-long ramp. The platform displayed beautiful masonry and contained a burial vault under its ramp. Nothing like it remained in all Polynesia, even though the statue it had once supported had fallen. As they excavated the great ahu at Vinapu, they found that the beautiful original stonework dated to about A.D 380, with less skillful additions at two later periods. Nearby, they uncovered a statue unlike all the others on the island. It was made from a square-cut red column just like the figure of Kon-Tiki that Heyerdahl had copied from Lake Titicaca. The ahu masonry and the statue style proved that the first Easter Islanders came from South America. The date shows that it was the first island in Polynesia to be inhabited.

The islanders eventually used their masonry skills to develop their own style. After the first European visitors, they had built bigger statues (such as the largest unfinished heads) until the statue making ended when the Short Ears invaded from the Gambier Islands twelve hundred miles west. The Long Ears retreated to the Poike Peninsula and built a defensive trench. They set the trench on fire, but the Short Ears sneaked behind their lines. The Long Ears died in their own fire. Only one Long Ear, Ororoina, survived, and his few descendants eleven generations later included the mayor of Easter Island.

Heyerdahl dug at the trench called "Iko's Ditch" or the "Long Ears Earth Oven" and found beautiful stonework lining the trench filled with the charred remains of the fire. After Captain Cook, European visitors found that the statues had been toppled over. This was due to wars among the Short Ears. In fact, there were times when all the families had to live in underground caves to avoid being killed. Heyerdahl's trench and cave discoveries silenced the naturalists who had scoffed at the tribal legends and taboos.

Each family stored its *akuaku* stones and images in their cave. These ancestral shares were sacred and often represented fearsome spirits. The cave also contained bones of the ancestors. Usually only the eldest man knew the cave's location, with its camouflaged entrance. The caves and their contents were taboo—prohibited from public use, display, or even comment. In fact, the very term *taboo* comes from Polynesia, and it came into English from Captain Cook's journal.

Heyerdahl achieved a great victory in anthropology in gaining the trust of natives so that they showed him taboo caves and akuakus. They also brought him rongo-rongo tablets from their caves. The lettering reverses and turns upside down at the end of each line—but Heyerdahl could not read it. That was reserved for Thomas Barthel to decipher around 1960, and he translates them as prayers and rituals mixed with legends.

Heyerdahl also found that some akuaku had images of bird men, such as those painted on the rocks at Orongo, the ruined village of the bird men overlooking the crater of Rano Kau. Each year the best athletes would compete to be the first to swim the shark-infested waters to the islet of Motu Nui and return with the first egg of the terns that nest there. This feat would determine the Bird-Man of the year.

As they continued digging Heyerdahl learned more about the statues. The excavations revealed statue bodies down to the waist. Some had long fingers wrapped around a big belly, a feature in common with statues both in Bolivia and in other parts of Polynesia. Heyerdahl watched for eighteen days as twelve men pried up a stone head with poles in order to slide rocks under it. They kept wedging stones underneath until the growing pile tilted the statue into upright position. Later, Heyerdahl and his excavation team watched in amazement as the mayor led 180 men to drag a twelve-ton statue rapidly across the plain, using the age-old technique.

In 1988, Easter Island became part of the country of Chile. Airplane flights from Chile now bring visitors twenty-six hundred miles west across the Pacific Ocean to see the mysterious island of statues, legends, caves, ahus, and rongo-rongo.

ANGKOR WAT, ANGKOR, CAMBODIA

After days of pushing through the jungle, Father Charles Emile Bouillevaux stared in awe at the largest temple in the world. Though it had ruined and reclaimed the vast complex, the jungle could not hide the size and grandeur of Angkor Wat. The French missionary wandered among the deserted ruins, admiring the architecture, towers, and carvings. Kings, gods, dancers, and seven-headed cobras adorned the walls. Battle scenes showed that elephants had been the heavy artillery. Bouillevaux had heard rumors of a vast ancient city and temple complex while passing through Cambodia, but no one knew how old it was or who had built it. Bouillevaux's search ended in 1850. Now he knew that the stories were true.

Ten years later, the French naturalist Henri Mouhot trekked along the eighty-seven-mile-long lake Tonle Sap and turned north to reach the ruined city. Mouhot wrote of the ruins, "It is grander than anything left to us by Greece or Rome." He too inquired about the builders, but no one knew. All stories claimed that either giants or gods had built it.

French archaeologists began to study the ruins in 1866, though they did not try to restore and preserve them until 1898. They studied the Chinese, Moslem, and Indian histories, together with the Sanskrit and Khmer inscriptions. By the time war forced them to leave in 1973, they had pieced together the chronology of its rulers. The Chinese called the region Fu Nan (or Phnom), now called Cambodia. Around A.D. 550, the Chenla took over. In the 700s, a king of Java conquered the area but was conquered in turn by the Khmer.

When Jayavarman II threw off the yoke of Javanese rule in 802, he proclaimed himself an incarnation of the Hindu god Shiva, established the Khmer Empire at Angkor, and set the example for elaborate temple building. After him, the Khmer Empire lasted six hundred years under a dynasty of thirty kings. His nephew, Indravarman, took the throne in 877 and built a fitting capital. He built a larger temple and dug canals and reservoirs to control the floods of the Mekong River and to retain some of the flood water until the dry season. His son, Yasovarman, continued the building process and built a temple-tomb for his father in the middle of a reservoir at Roluos.

In the twelfth century, Suryavarman II extended the Khmer Empire considerably. He ruled from the China Sea to the Indian Ocean. As his domain grew, so did his capital city, Angkor. By the end of his reign, around 1150, the capital complex may have housed a million people, the largest city in the world at the time.

The huge temple of Angkor Wat was the king's last great building project, which he began about 1113. The surrounding moat covered an area of over 3.5 square miles. The alligator-infested moat was five hundred feet wide in the front, and citizens crossed the moat on a causeway thirty feet wide. At the end of the causeway, everyone passed through the entry tower.

Beyond the entry, the stone walk continues past smaller buildings and basins toward the main temple. Angkor Wat is the largest temple at Angkor and forms a rectangle six hundred feet wide (two football fields) and seven hundred feet long. Its five domes (pagodas) rise above the highest of three tiers. Four identical domes stand in each corner, and a larger one rises in the center. The large dome is about two hundred feet high for a total height of seven hundred feet above the base of the lowest tier. Smaller cross-shaped buildings with corbel arches, now called libraries, stand on the lower tiers.

A colonnade encloses the lowest tier. In the front, the columns form one side of a roofed hallway, and the wall on the other side of the hallway is carved in raised relief (called bas relief). Including other passages in the temple, bas reliefs decorate over one thousand feet of the walls in the temple. The thousands of carvings depict warriors, elephants, dancers, and royal figures. These carvings remind worshipers entering the temple of the history of the world according to Hinduism and Khmer culture. Suryavarman II dedicated the temple to the god Vishnu, whose eight-foot statue stands at an entrance.

Some thirty years later, Jayavarman VII added many buildings and brought the construction at Angkor to a close. He built an even larger temple complex at Angkor Thom, only a mile away from Angkor Wat and also part of the city of Angkor. This square complex, also surrounded by a moat, extended three miles on each side. However, none of its temples reached the height or magnificence of Angkor Wat. He also built a number of other temples in the vicinity.

In 1181 Jayavarman VII also converted the city from Hinduism to Buddhism. This explains the Hall of one thousand

Library at Angkor Wat

Elephant combat in carved relief

Buddhas on the first tier of Angkor Wat. Opposite this hall is a Hall of Echoes, which has acoustics that make echoes for even the smallest sound, such as the thumping of your chest.

In 1296 the Chinese historian Chou Ta-kuan visited Angkor at the height of its glory. His memoirs, *Notes on the Customs of Cambodia,* is the only firsthand account of life at Angkor. By this time, smiling faces of Lokesvara, an incarnation of Buddha, adorned the newer buildings. Chou Ta-kuan saw the dingy peasant huts and the fine stone mansions of princes. He saw much gold in the city: gold lion statues flanking a gold bridge, a gold tower, and a golden crown worn by the king.

Chou, as an ambassador, received the privilege of seeing the king. After waiting for some time with princes and paupers alike, seashell trumpets announced one of the two daily royal audiences. When the curtain rose, Chou saw the king through a gold-framed window. Chou quickly bowed to the floor until the trumpeting stopped. Then he looked up again to bask in the royal splendor. Besides the golden crown, the king wore garlands of jasmine, bracelets loaded with pearls, golden anklets, and rings inlaid with gems. However, the finery that Chou witnessed perished in 1431, when the Thai besieged Angkor for

Moat and entrance gates with distant temple towers

seven months and raided it, taking away all that they could carry after their victory. They returned for more plunder later, but it was empty. No one knows where the myriad of people went.

Today, visitors can reach Angkor Wat on international flights to Phnom Penh and a connecting flight to Siemreap at the northwest end of Tonle Sap. A taxi takes passengers the final four miles north to Angkor Wat.

Angkor was the biggest temple complex ever made. It consisted of one thousand temples covering 120 square miles. However, the jungle has taken its toll on the brick of the oldest temples. Many have completely disintegrated; only traces remain of others. Even some stone temples have been covered completely by vegetation. Many of the reservoirs, canals, and moats have dried up, and some of the statues have been stolen or vandalized. Nevertheless, tourists can still visit thirty-nine temples. Angkor Wat is the largest and most beautiful of the temples in this vast complex, and it is the largest Hindu temple ever built.

MACHU PICCHU, CUZCO, PERU

Hiram Bingham had trudged for a couple of days from Cuzco, the ancient Inca capital, along the banks of the Urubamba River. He had asked the few people he passed for directions to Vilcabamba, but no one knew what he meant.

"You want to see ruins?" responded the next poor farmer to Bingham's inquiry. He pointed at a distant cliff top fifteen hundred feet above the river, perched between two craggy peaks. "I can take you up there to Machu Picchu." Bingham, an adventurous explorer from Yale University, agreed immediately. They went together, sometimes pushing their way through thick jungle and sometimes crossing deep chasms on rope suspension bridges. Finally, they struggled up the last steep climb to the plateau.

Fine stonework at Machu Picchu

Bingham wandered for hours among the five acres of pure white granite buildings: dwellings for fifteen hundred people, temples, palaces, tombs, and terraces for crops covered with dirt hauled up from the valley. The stones of the buildings were cut and fitted so well that even though no mortar held them together, earthquakes of the last centuries had not toppled them. Bingham could not even slide his knife blade between the stones. The stonework still testified to an advanced civilization.

Bingham marveled at the stonework and recalled what he had read about the Incas. He knew that Inca civilization began around A.D. 1100. The rulers had laid out the great capital city, Cuzco, in the shape of a puma, with the royal fortress, Sacsahuaman, at the head. By 1438, under the reign of Pachacuti, Inca civilization had expanded enough to be called an empire. Topa, his successor, extended the empire to its furthest limits two thousand miles along the Pacific coast. The excellent communication system knit the empire together. Flagstone roads crossed the empire, making it easy for armies and messengers to travel, whether by llama or on foot. Where the terrain would not permit a stone path, vine bridges or tunnels were employed. By providing rest houses for messengers to run in relays, messages could travel two hundred miles a day. Though they had no writing, the Incas coded messages using different colors of wool and different sizes and numbers of knots. However, two factions were struggling for supremacy, and the civil strife had weakened the empire.

In 1532 the Spanish conquistador Francisco Pizarro invaded and conquered the Incas during this time of weakness. By 1572, when Tupac Amaru was executed, Spanish domination was complete. Pizarro's historian left detailed descriptions of each city that they visited before the Spanish plundered it. When they conquered Cuzco, they took the sacred virgins, but one hundred of them had already escaped. The Spanish also heard of Vilcabamba, where Manco Capac, the last Inca emperor, hid for thirty-six years. However, they never located the last refuge of the emperor.

Bingham had come to Peru hoping to solve the mysteries of what had happened to the emperor and to the one hundred virgins and to locate the elusive city of Vilcabamba. Now in 1911 he had found a city easily defensible and high in the mountains

that did not match any of the Spanish records. He was sure he had found the last refuge of the Incas who had eluded the Spanish. Bingham admired the Incas' beautiful work with soft metals: gold, silver, copper, and bronze. Machu Picchu gave him a new appreciation for Inca stone masonry. Each stone was hauled up the mountain, perfectly cut, and fitted into place, all without the benefit of machinery or even iron tools. It must have taken a long time, even with a huge labor force.

Machu Picchu remains a mystery. When and why was it built? Some scholars think it was built as the first Inca capital. Others think that it served primarily for religious purposes. Certainly it does have a temple and a ring that symbolized the tether for the sun. Bingham thought it was built as the last fortress against the Spaniards, known as Vilcabamba, but the true location of Vilcabamba has since been found deep in the Amazon jungle. However, its location near Cuzco and its size suggests that it may indeed have been the refuge of the one hundred virgins. Quite probably the one hundred lost virgins escaped to Machu Picchu. Escape to a sacred city would be natural for sacred virgins who served in the Temple of the Sun. If so, they would have lived out their lives at Machu Picchu and would have been buried in its tombs.

While the mysteries that drew Bingham to Peru have mostly been solved, his discovery of Machu Picchu poses new mysteries. Why would such a strong fortress city decline? Perhaps the king simply abandoned it for a new and more convenient capital at Cuzco. Perhaps its citizens died in the Inca civil war. Victorious Inca factions executed all the citizens of the defeated city. Even the name of the city is a mystery. No one knows its ancient name. The modern name, Machu Picchu,

Intihuatana, the tether for the sun

simply means "Old Peak," referring to the nearby mountain summit. The Spanish recorded their conquests of the major Inca cities and at least recorded the rumors they heard of Vilcabamba—but of Machu Picchu their records are silent.

Today, Machu Picchu sits precariously on a plateau at an elevation of 7,875 feet on the east slopes of the Andes Mountains, sixty miles northwest of Cuzco. Visitors can take international flights to Lima, the capital of Peru, and then domestic flights to Cuzco. From Cuzco, trains and buses run to a station near Machu Picchu, but the last part of the journey requires a few hours of steep uphill walking. An additional option for adventure is to hike the old Inca Trail from Cuzco to Machu Picchu.

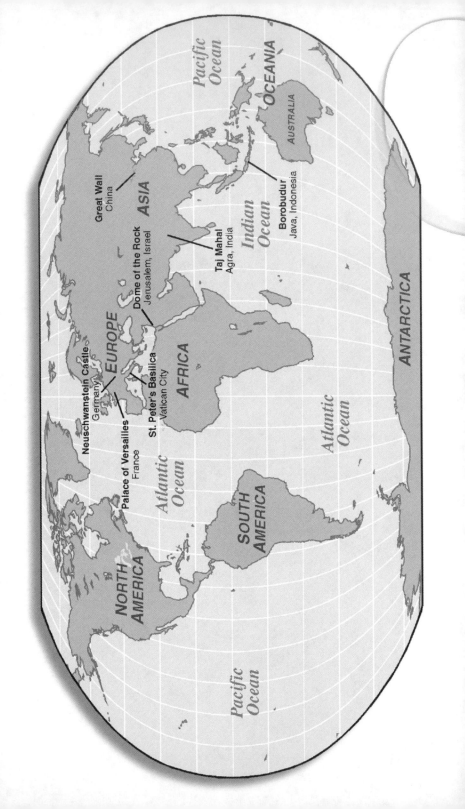

Seven

architectural

Wonders

7 The Seven Architectural Wonders

The architectural wonders span the gap between the archaeological wonders and the technological wonders of the world. All were built before the twentieth century, and all are presently in use. The oldest of these wonders is the Great Wall of China. The most recent is Neuschwanstein Castle, built in the 1880s. The list also includes the largest and most famous of all the tombs, palaces, cathedrals, temples, and mosques. All seven appear on the chapter opener map.

Hillman Travel lists the seven modern wonders of the world according to the most votes from thousands of world travelers. This list provides the seven most highly acclaimed places to visit worldwide: the Colosseum of Rome, the Grand Canyon, the Great Wall of China, Machu Picchu, the Pyramids, Serengeti, and the Taj Mahal. While some of these are ancient, archaeological or natural wonders, the Great Wall and the Taj Mahal clearly rank among the seven architectural wonders of the world.

The Taj Mahal is clearly the most acclaimed architectural wonder. It is not only on the list from Hillman Travel but also on the lists of the seven modern wonders of the world by Viewmaster and Thomas (see Chapter Two). St. Peter's Basilica was also included by Lowell Thomas (see list in Chapter Two).

All seven wonders of architecture display God's mercy toward sinful man. Two of the buildings were built at great expense by selfish, indulgent kings—a palace by Louis XIV and a castle by King Ludwig. Two others were also built by extravagant rulers. Shah Jahan built a tomb to excel all others, and the emperor who built the Great Wall sought a monument worthy of his proud reign. The other three wonders are centers for false religious systems.

God could send natural disasters such as earthquakes to destroy these monuments, but instead He sends rain upon both the just and the unjust. God demonstrates patience toward the pride of man during this life, but there is a day of judgment coming. God "is longsuffering to us-ward, not willing that any should perish, but that all should come to repentance" (II Pet. 3:9). "But Thou, O Lord, art a God full of compassion, and gracious, longsuffering, and plenteous in mercy and truth" (Ps. 86:15).

GREAT WALL OF CHINA

"The Mongol horsemen have raided us again," said Meng Tian, the emperor's most successful general. Emperor Qin Shihuangdi, the first emperor over all of China, made an instant decision. "This must stop. Build a wall." Meng Tian began work about 214 B.C. with three hundred thousand laborers, including peasants, soldiers, and prisoners. The project took ten years.

Emperor Qin had inherited his father's kingdom at age thirteen, and by 221 B.C. at age thirty-eight, he had created an empire by subduing the feuding kingdoms around him. The emperor ordered all the books to be burned (except his imperial library). He killed 460 disobedient scholars and forced many more to work on the wall. His reign of terror provoked several assassination attempts from Chinese workers at the cost of their own lives. With forced labor, Qin had a great palace built for himself, a ten-thousand-seat hall, long canals, roads, and palaces for each of his wives.

The wall consists of solid dirt on stone foundations and was adorned with bricks on the outside. The king killed inefficient and lazy workers and threw the thousands of bodies into the wall as fill. The heavy death toll explains why many call the wall the Wall of Tears and the Longest Graveyard on Earth.

When completed, the wall was twenty-five feet thick at the base and eighteen feet thick at the top. The wall stands thirty feet high, and the twenty-five thousand towers and fifteen thousand watchtowers along the wall rise an additional ten feet. Soldiers marched ten abreast and cavalry rode five abreast along the road on top to defend China against Mongol hordes. Smoke signals during the day and huge bonfires at night communicated messages quickly along the wall.

The wall stretches about fifteen hundred miles from end to end as the crow flies (as far as New York City to Fargo, North Dakota). It begins near the east coast of China at Beijing, winds

through the mountains, plunges down ravines and across great rivers, marches across swamps, and ends at Kiayu Kuan in the Gobi Desert. Including all the curves, parallel

Soldiers on patrol

stretches, and offshoots that the soldiers patrolled, the wall runs 3,946 miles, according to the Chinese government. However, a Chinese man who recently walked the entire wall measured it with a pedometer and found it to be 4,163 miles long, or as far as Chicago to Paris.

During periods of peace, the wall fell into disrepair. In A.D. 607, when attacks renewed, the Sui dynasty repaired the wall. Perhaps five hundred thousand workers labored this time, half of whom died. Again, in the 1400s, the Ming dynasty instituted another rebuilding program. Since some breaches in the wall have not been repaired in modern times, the wall is no longer continuous.

In 1994, scientists on the space shuttle orbiting the earth at a distance of over one thousand miles spotted the Great Wall. It is the only man-made feature that can be seen from that great distance. The scientists also recognized traces of an older section of the wall by studying radar images of a section 430 miles west of Beijing. The older dirt mounds from the Sui dynasty run parallel to the present wall of the Ming dynasty. The later builders must have decided to build a new section here instead of trying to repair the old one.

Visitors to the wall today can fly to Beijing and then take a bus about fifty miles or so to either Badaling Pass or Mutianyu. These two sections of the wall have been restored to their ancient appearance. Many visitors enjoy the train tours and helicopter tours from Beijing as well. Some visitors prefer the unmaintained sections of the wall to avoid crowds and commercialization. All visitors admire the ancient wall, one of the oldest remaining man-made structures. Since its immensity makes it the only man-made object visible from space, the Great Wall of China clearly deserves a place among the wonders of the world.

BOROBUDUR, JAVA, INDONESIA

Borobudur, on the island of Java in Indonesia, is the largest structure in the Southern Hemisphere. The two million stones used in its construction form terraces that rise to a height of 1,310 feet. The lowest terrace is about 360 feet long on each side. This towering structure far surpasses the size of the central temples of the other major religions of the world. It is also the highest of all the architectural wonders. The name *Borobudur* means many Buddhas. The temple is still the largest Buddhist temple. Indonesian literature includes it among the Seven Wonders of the World.

The Sailendra dynasty built the temple around the year 800 using a gray volcanic stone. They took advantage of a small hill to make the terraces easier to build. After two centuries the temple fell into disuse, and for over nine hundred years the jungle reclaimed the site. However, in 1814, while English troops occupied Java, an army officer discovered the ruins in the jungle. A century later, from 1907-11, Dutch archaeologists began clearing the site, and in the 1970s and 1980s a United Nations program helped to complete the restorations. Since its restoration, it has again become a center of Buddhist worship.

The five lowest terraces form squares with a stairway to the next level in the center of each side. Because Buddhists associate the counter-clockwise direction with evil, visitors must enter from the

Approaching Borobudur

135

Carving of Buddha teaching disciples

east and walk clockwise around each terrace before ascending to the next. As visitors walk around the temple, they see 436 statues of Buddha set in niches and some fifteen hundred panels carved in relief. On the lowest levels, scenes depict life in Java in the ninth century, from work and family life to dancers and ships at sea. Higher levels depict the life of Buddha, the deeds of Buddha, and beliefs of Buddhism.

The three highest terraces are circular. The contrast with the square terraces is intentional because the higher terraces represent the spiritual journey. Whereas the more numerous square terraces are richly adorned to depict the material world, the circular terraces are sparsely decorated to suggest the spiritual world of the Buddhas. Each circular terrace has bell-shaped structures called *stupas*. All the stupas are the same size and

Five square and three circular tiers of Borobudur

contain a life-size Buddha statue, which visitors can see through the latticed design of the bell. Each of the seventy-two Buddhas has its hands in a different position with symbolic meaning for Buddhists.

In the center of the top terrace is a huge stupa fifty feet in diameter. This one also contains a statue of Buddha, but it is completely enclosed to prevent viewing. This stupa represents nirvana. Buddhists mistakenly think *nirvana* will bring an end to thought. By the time the pilgrim has walked around all the terraces, he has walked about three miles. The design well represents the religion—walking by one's own effort in circles leading to an unreachable goal.

To visit the amazing architecture of Borobudur, visitors can fly to Jakarta, the capital of Indonesia, and then board a connecting flight or a train to Yogyakarta near the center of the island of Java. From here, regular buses run twenty-six miles northeast to Borobudur.

THE TAJ MAHAL, AGRA, INDIA

Shah Jahan expected news of his new child. Mumtaz Mahal, his faithful wife for eighteen years, was in labor for the fourteenth time. Shah Jahan was born Prince Kurram on January 5, 1592, in Lahore. When his father, Emperor Jahangir, died in 1627, Shah Jahan had become emperor of all India. In 1612 he had married Arjumand Banu Baygam, but now in 1629 she was called Mumtaz Mahal, or

Reflections at dusk

"Chosen of the Palace"—the name of his favorite wife.

"Emperor!" The scurrying messengers interrupted his contented reverie. Their voices quavered. "Emperor! Your child lives, but not your wife." The news pierced him like a javelin, and he grieved for two full years. He determined to build for his wife a tomb at Agra surpassing all the buildings in the world. For twenty-two years, 20,000 men worked on the tomb. The emperor succeeded because today all recognize the Taj Mahal as the pinnacle of Mogul architecture, and many call it the most beautiful building in the world. Part of his wife's name, Mahal, was used in naming the tomb.

The tomb of white marble rests on a red sandstone platform. The tomb itself, 186 feet long on each side, would cover more than half a football field. The large archways rise as high as a *Gemini* spacecraft, 109 feet, and the great dome adds another 120 feet to the total height. The white marble, quarried two hundred miles away, is inlaid with precious stones. Black marble calligraphy decorates the tomb with quotations from the Koran. The prayer towers, called minarets, at each corner of the platform stand 133 feet high. The garden setting, the still waters of

the reflecting pools, and the Jumna River add to the beauty and serenity of this tomb.

In later years the shah extended his Mogul Empire, founded Delhi, and built the Peacock Throne. However, the sins of his youth found him out. Just as he had rebelled against his father, his son Aurangzeb deposed him in 1658. While still imprisoned in the fort at Agra, he died on January 22, 1666. The shah is buried with his wife in the Taj Mahal.

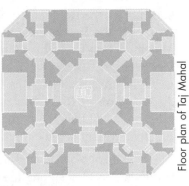

Floor plan of Taj Mahal

Agra and the Taj Mahal are 120 miles from Delhi, a three-hour drive. The numerous domestic flights available to Agra and the scores of riders on the Taj Express rail line from Delhi to Agra indicate the extreme popularity of the Taj Mahal.

DOME OF THE ROCK, JERUSALEM, ISRAEL

According to Islam, Muhammad dismounted from his steed, Burak, which the archangel Gabriel had given him. Muhammad recognized the Rock of Abraham, upon which Abraham had prepared to offer Isaac. On this rock, the foundation stone of the whole world, Muhammad knelt and prayed. After praying, Muhammad ascended to heaven from the Rock of Abraham while seated on his horse, Burak.

Islam, the religion of the Muslims, considers Muhammad to be the greatest prophet in history. Muhammad lived from about A.D. 570-632 and founded the religion of Islam. Since the Muslims believe that Muhammad ascended to heaven after kneeling on the Rock of Abraham, they regard the rock as sacred; only the Kaaba stone in Mecca is considered more sacred. Muslim caliph Umar I (or Omar I) of Arabia took over Jerusalem in A.D. 638. In A.D. 691 the caliph Abdel Malik finished the construction of the Mosque of Omar, usually called the Dome of the Rock. Muhammad is buried in the Prophet's Mosque in Medina, the third most holy site in Islam. In 969 Egyptian Muslims took control of Jerusalem.

The Mosque of Omar is the oldest remaining Muslim building. It is also among the largest, and it is certainly the most beautiful. Because it is the pinnacle of Islamic architecture, it is sometimes called the "Jewel of Islam." The mosque's dome is 65 feet in diameter and 110 feet high. The golden dome is topped with an emblem of Islam. The wooden dome rests on a circular drum, which rises above the eight 60-foot long, 36-foot high walls forming the lower octagonal building. Mosaics, marble, blue-glazed tiles, and quotations from the Koran in calligraphy adorn the exterior.

While the story of Muhammad's ascension is a legend, the stone does represent the probable site of the story of Abraham and Isaac. The Bible says that the event occurred on Mt. Moriah (Gen. 22:2). When Omar took Jerusalem, the temple of God had been in ruins since 70 A.D., when the Romans destroyed it. Omar, therefore, dug down in the ruins to find the original stone. The Romans had not left one stone of the temple upon another—just as the Lord had said (Matt. 24:1-2), but they left the western foundation as a reminder of their victory. This exposed foundation, now called the Western Wall, is the last vestige of the temple and is sacred to Jews. Christians take interest in Christ's tomb nearby. (More on

Dome of the Rock above the Wailing Wall

Christian sites is in the Epilogue at the end of this book.) In the mosque, Muslims are more interested in Muhammad's footprint and the three hairs from his beard, but the Rock of Abraham itself has historical interest for Christians and Jews, though not as an object of worship.

The Muslim rulers of Jerusalem were tolerant of Christians and Jews until the eleventh century, when they began to destroy Christian holy places. This destruction provoked the Crusades. Europe reconquered Jerusalem in 1099, but Saladin recaptured it for Islam in 1187. Although there were several more attempts in the Holy Wars to get it back, Muslims held Jerusalem from 1244 to 1917, when the British took the city. Arabs took the city briefly in 1948, just before the new nation of Israel captured it. It became the capital for Israel in 1950. Through most of this time, Muslims, Jews, and Christians have tolerated each other at the various holy sites.

Since Jerusalem has sites sacred to all three of the world's major monotheistic religions, pilgrims from all over the world

Sunrise over Jerusalem. Note the smaller al-Aqsa mosque (left) with its sacred black dome.

travel there. Most visitors take international flights to Ben Gurion Airport in Tel Aviv (adjacent to ancient Joppa). Buses, taxis, or rental cars permit easy transport along the thirty-mile drive from the Mediterranean coast to the twenty-five hundred foot elevation of Jerusalem. The temple is inside the walls of the old city of Jerusalem. Because the centuries-old streets are not intended for cars, visitors should plan on walking to the mosque. Visitors must also follow protocol at the various holy sites. For example, Christian sites require visitors to remove hats, whereas Jews at the most holy area along the Western Wall require men to don a special cap. Those who enter the mosque to see the Rock of Abraham must remove their shoes.

ST PETER'S BASILICA, ROME, VATICAN CITY

Like the Muslims, Catholics also put forth efforts to build architectural masterpieces. What cathedrals match the Dome of the Rock for splendor? Among the more famous are those at

Amiens, Bourges, Canterbury, Chartres, Cologne, Durham, Lincoln, London, Milan, Moscow, Notre Dame, Paris, Rheims, Salisbury, Seville, Strasbourg, Ulm, Venice, and York. Outside Europe there are famous cathedrals at Montreal, New York, New Orleans, Mexico City, and throughout Latin America.

Vatican City, however, has the most famous cathedral, which is named after the famous apostle—St. Peter's Basilica. Its fame rests on three points: its significance in the religion, its architects, and its size. Its significance in marking the grave of the apostle Peter, whom Catholics claim as their first pope, strengthens its position as the mother church for all Catholics. Its architecture equals or surpasses all other cathedrals since it includes the work of many great masters, such as Michelangelo. In size, it remains among the largest in the world.

The Bible does not say what happened to Peter, except that he would die a martyr's death (John 21:18-19). Tradition says that Peter was crucified by Nero in Rome. Since Peter did not feel worthy to die the same death as his Lord, he requested to be crucified upside down. If this tradition is accurate, he would have been buried in Rome around A.D. 64. Modern excavations beneath the cathedral have located both an ancient graveyard and prayers to Peter that were etched in stone near an unmarked tomb. These findings suggest that at least one ancient Roman thought that Peter was buried there, though no more conclusive proof has been found.

Emperor Constantine built a basilica around the grave in A.D. 325. Pope Nicholas V called for extensive renovations, which were not completed due to his death in 1455. In 1506 Pope Julius II recognized the need to replace the cathedral completely with a grand structure to act as the central church of Catholicism.

Inside St. Peter's Basilica

Unfortunately, all of the next eight architects died before its completion: Bramante in 1514, Raphael in 1520, Sangallo the Elder in 1535, Sangallo the Younger in 1546, Michelangelo in 1564, Ligorio in 1583, Fontana in 1597, and della Porta in 1602.

Finally, the architect Maderno completed it, and Pope Urban VIII made the official dedication on November 18, 1626. It was della Porta who completed the dome designed by Michelangelo, and Maderno gave the building its final shape and front. Thirty years later the architect Bernini, who decorated much of the interior in baroque style, added the huge entrance plaza with its colonnades of 284 columns.

St. Peter's Basilica was the largest cathedral in the world when it was built and remained so for centuries. The building, shaped like a cross, covers 240,000 square feet, giving it a floor space of fifteen football fields. The longest dimension is 700 feet, and the width at the cross part is 450 feet. The dome

crowns the
building at the
point where the
aisles cross, ris-
ing 435 feet
high and having
a diameter of
180 feet.

Tallest Cathedrals		
cathedral	year	height
Ulm, Germany (first)	1419	446
St. Peter's, Vatican City	1602	448
Strasbourg, France	1400s	466
St. Nicholas, Germany	—	473
Cologne, Germany	1880	511
Notre Dame, Cote d'Ivoire	1990	518
Ulm, Germany (newer)	1890	528

Although the spire of Ulm Cathedral in Germany rises higher
(528 feet), its overall size does not exceed St. Peter's. In 1990
the Basilica of Notre Dame in Yamoussoukro, Cote d'Ivoire,
Africa, was completed to rival the diameter of St. Peter's dome.

Visitors can ascend to view the dome's lantern from a balcony in St. Peter's or descend beneath the altar to view the
cemetery excavations. All visitors want to see Michelangelo's
statue *Pietà,* which depicts Mary holding the corpse of Jesus.
More of Michelangelo's work, including the *Last Supper,* can be
seen on the main wall and ceiling of the Sistine Chapel. Airline
flights to Rome and public ground transportation provide easy
access to the Vatican City.

PALACE OF VERSAILLES, FRANCE

"I am the State," said Louis XIV. He tolerated no other authority in France. Those desiring audience with the king knew
that they had no chance without seeking his favor. Since he had
chosen the sun as his symbol, his favorite name was Sun King;
but he also enjoyed the titles God-given, Louis the Great, and
Grand Monarch. These reflected his hope to be the greatest
monarch in all of Europe. The king looked at the small chateau
from which his father had set out on hunts. "That's not a hunt-

The Hall of Mirrors

ing lodge fit for the greatest of kings," he thought. The large palaces at the Louvre and the Tuileries seemed commonplace. As he envisioned one far larger, he began to formulate plans to build a new palace.

Work began in 1661, but construction required twenty-one years before King Louis XIV and his court could move in. Louis Le Vau and later Jules Hardouin Mansart served as architects. One side is 2,100 feet long (over one-third of a mile). The great Hall of Mirrors has seventeen windows along one side that are matched on the other side by mirrors. Paintings by Charles Lebrun, completed around 1678, flattered the king's pride by depicting "heroic" events in his reign. Inscriptions and other monuments also honored his greatness. Even before the building was complete, French nobles enjoyed visiting the gardens and viewing the landscaping designed by André Le Notre. The beautiful gardens encompassed many fountains, lakes, a grand canal, and a "Little Venice." Some areas provided parklike settings for walks. Other portions offered scenic views and statues by sculptors such as Coysevox,

Foggini, Girardon, Le Hongre, Marsy, Regnaudin, and Tuby. Some of the flower bed arrangements formed patterns and shapes. In 1664, 1668, and 1674, the gardens served as the setting for operas and plays by such famous writers as Lully and Molière.

All of the king's extravagant buildings and greed required great taxes, and his wars to reclaim lands that had once been owned by France sent the nation into debt. Even with so much splendor about him, he felt no gratitude to law-abiding taxpayers who made it possible. One such group of hard-working skilled laborers, the Huguenots, were Protestant Christians who had fled Catholic persecution in many European countries a century before. They had been protected in France by the Edict of Nantes since 1598. King Louis XIV revoked the edict in 1685, and two hundred thousand Huguenots fled for their lives.

When Louis XIV died in 1715, his successors expanded the palace and gardens even farther, offering no relief to the taxpayers. Louis XV made Versailles a symbol of luxury. His architect Gabriel added more rooms and gardens, an opera salon, and a smaller palace called the Petit Trianon. Louis XVI added the library and spent his time hunting. Marie Antoinette built a theater and a rustic hamlet where she could act out the role of a peasant. She ignored the financial crisis facing France and indulged her whims. She fired court advisors who tried to reduce spending. A popular anecdote epitomized her haughty disregard for the people. She asked an advisor why the people were angry. Hearing that they lacked bread, she replied "Let them eat cake!"

After more than one hundred years of heavy taxation, the French people rebelled. The French Revolution targeted Versailles as the hated symbol of luxury in 1789.

Latona Fountain at Versailles

Mobs stormed the palace, destroyed much furniture and art, and forced Louis XVI and Marie Antoinette to move to the Tuileries, the smaller palace in Paris. After the king and queen attempted to escape and later revealed military secrets to foreign powers, they were both guillotined in 1793.

The hated palace remained vacant after the revolution. In 1870, the Germans used it for their military base in attacking Paris during the Franco-Prussian War. Restoration of the palace began in the early 1900s. Now, many of the thirteen hundred rooms appear as they did when the royal family lived there. The 250 acres of gardens complement the extensive palace/museum. Flights to Paris and an eleven-mile train ride southwest make the palace easy to visit. It is one of the most visited sites in Europe.

NEUSCHWANSTEIN CASTLE, GERMANY

Dashing young King Ludwig of Bavaria savored the fading sounds of the opera *Tannhäuser*. His artificial cave looked remarkably realistic with an underground lake amidst its stalagmites and stalactites. The cave room, or Venusberg Grotto, also had a huge painting of a scene from the opera and excellent acoustics to enhance his enjoyment. As he applauded the performance, he glanced at the overweight singer Madame Scheffzky, who stood in the swan-shaped boat in the middle of the lake. Suddenly Madame Scheffzky fell into the lake. Her "fall" was obviously intentional; she hoped the king would come to her rescue. "Fetch Madame Scheffzky and escort her to the door," Ludwig directed his servant. No such pettiness would again ruin his operas.

Although the king had been born in Nymphenburg Castle, Munich, on August 25, 1845, he lived most of his life at Hohenschwangau Castle (a tenth-century castle on Alpen Lake, which his father had restored). His father had also planned to rebuild a castle nearby that would offer a better view of the lake and the mountains from a higher vantage point. However, his father died when Ludwig was nineteen. Ludwig became king on March 10, 1864.

The paintings depicting legends of Lohengrin, the Knight of the Swan, at his father's castle as well as a performance of Wagner's opera *Lohengrin* left deep impressions on Ludwig. After ascending the throne, Ludwig summoned Wagner and offered to finance his musical work. Later, in 1868, Ludwig revealed to Wagner his plan to carry out his father's idea: "I have the intention to rebuild the ancient castle ruins of Schwanstein near the Poellat Gorge in the true style of the ancient German

knights' castles. The place is one of the nicest ever found." Construction began the following year, inspired by a painting of a castle by Christian Jank, a German painter and set designer.

Ludwig began building Neuschwanstein Castle in 1869. In 1874 he began building a second castle, Castle Linderhof, with its Venusberg Grotto. It was finished in 1878. Immediately, he began yet another castle, Castle Herrenchiemsee. This

Murals and a gold table setting adorn the dining room.

third castle showed the influence of Versailles on King Ludwig. He modeled rooms after the Hall of Mirrors and the bedroom of King Louis XIV. Though Louis XIV had died over 150 years before, Ludwig reserved the bedroom for the former king's use, and he once reportedly had dinner with King Louis's ghost. In 1886 Ludwig completed Neuschwanstein Castle after seventeen years of work and moved in. As his third castle neared completion, he prepared for breaking ground for a fourth castle, Castle Falkenstein.

Some of his subjects called him the Mad King. They questioned Ludwig's sanity because of his many castles and his obsession with medieval mythology, but his strangeness regarding Louis XIV made them certain. On June 11, 1886, a commission from Munich declared him unfit to rule. After living at Neuschwanstein Castle only three months, his subjects took the king to Castle Berg at the edge of Starnberg Lake. He mysteriously drowned two days later—a probable suicide. When the king died, all construction halted, so the third castle was never

finished. No further castles were begun.

In spite of all his building, Ludwig built not only for himself but also for his heritage. His own name appears only once at Neuschwanstein (on a coat of arms in the Singer's Hall). The paintings and opera stages also preserved the national folklore. Perhaps for this reason, the luxurious castles were not hated by the people. Ludwig remains the favorite king of the

Bavarian people in spite of—or perhaps because of—his touch of insanity.

The many towers and balconies of Neuschwanstein Castle make it a classic for fairy-tale lovers. The interior decor more than satisfies visitors lured by the impressive exterior. Ascending the marble staircase to the vaulted vestibules, visitors pass through a marble entrance into the throne hall, decorated in Byzantine style with a gallery of columns, mosaic floor, and gold-covered brass chandelier. A painting of Christ above the raised area for the throne faces a painting of St. George and the Dragon. The balcony of the throne room looks out between arches over Alpen Lake and the castle of Ludwig's boyhood in the forest below.

The king's fascination with German legends resulted in a love for the legend-based operas by Richard Wagner. Scenes from the operas are painted on the walls all over the castle. Many of the paintings are murals that take up an entire wall. Such great painting tasks required many painters. Four rooms in the king's living quarters—the bedroom, living room, study, and dining room—contain Wagnerian scenes painted by Piloty, Heckel, Hauschild, and Aigner. The bedroom features *Tristan und Isolde;* the living room shows *Lohengrin;* the study,

Mural in Neuschwanstein Castle

Tannhäuser; and scenes from all three operas decorate the dining room. Chandeliers and ornately carved wood ceilings and floors also adorn each of these rooms. Fourteen sculptors carved for four and a half years to finish the oak furniture of the Neo-Gothic style bedroom with its embroidered coverings of Bavarian blue. Matching curtains veil the windows that look out on Poellat Gorge and its 149-foot-high waterfall. The living room and study in Romanesque style sport hand-embroidered silk curtains. A food lift brought food to the dining room from the kitchen three stories below.

Beautiful woodwork and stained glass by Mayer decorate the private chapel and prayer room. Stained glass scenes depict the king's namesake, King Ludwig IX of France, called the Saint. The dressing room displays paintings by Ille of a medieval lyric poet as well as scenes from Wagner's *Die Meistersinger.*

Ludwig was greatly impressed by Wartburg Castle in Thuringia. The Singer's Room at Neuschwanstein shows the most similarity to Wartburg Castle. At one end of the gallery stands a stage with a magic forest backdrop painted by Jank.

The remainder of the gallery, intended for those listening to the stage performances of Wagner, shows scenes by Speiss and Piloty from Wagner's *Parsifal*. Several chandeliers hang from the high paneled ceiling, and candelabras line the walls between paintings. Due to Ludwig's early death, concerts were not held there until 1933, at the fiftieth anniversary of Wagner's death. These concerts were held for only six years, but since 1969 concerts have been held each September.

Neuschwanstein Castle is the ultimate fairy-tale castle. Though not as old as the medieval castles, it surpasses them all in beauty, design, and fame. Visitors to the castle travel through the Bavarian Alps of Germany near the town of Füssen at the border of Austria. After parking at Castle Hohenschwangau, where Ludwig grew up, visitors walk one mile to Neuschwanstein Castle. Of the three castles built by Ludwig, Neuschwanstein is the masterpiece. It took the longest to build and is the most famous. While its name is not a household word, its image is familiar from calendars and puzzles worldide. In fact, Disney World in Florida selected the castle as a model for its own fairy-tale castle.

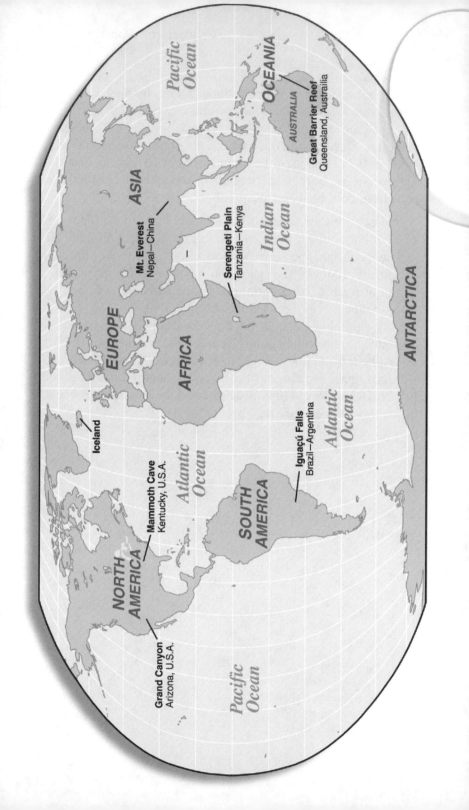

Pacific Ocean

OCEANIA

AUSTRALIA

Great Barrier Reef
Queensland, Australia

ASIA

Mt. Everest
Nepal—China

Serengeti Plain
Tanzania—Kenya

Indian Ocean

EUROPE

AFRICA

ANTARCTICA

Iceland

Atlantic Ocean

Atlantic Ocean

Mammoth Cave
Kentucky, U.S.A.

Iguaçu Falls
Brazil—Argentina

SOUTH AMERICA

NORTH AMERICA

Grand Canyon
Arizona, U.S.A.

Pacific Ocean

Seven

natural

Wonders

7 The Seven Natural Wonders

In addition to marvels of human achievement, authors have sometimes sought to identify the natural wonders of the world. Recognized for their natural beauty and breathtaking grandeur, such places are the most awesome sights in God's creation. Compare the following lists compiled by Lowell Thomas, Viewmaster, Natural Bridge, World Almanac, and George Bailey.

Thomas	View-Master	Natural Bridge	World Almanac	Bailey
Grand Canyon	Grand Canyon	Garden of the Gods	Grand Canyon	Grand Canyon
Ganges River	Carlsbad Caverns	Blue Grotto	Northern Lights	Caves in France and Spain
Mt. Fuji	Kilauea Volcano	Valley of 10,000 Smokes	Paricutin Volcano	Paricutin Volcano
Angel Falls	Old Faithful	Yellowstone	Mt. Everest	Mt. Everest
Victoria Falls	Angel Falls	Niagara Falls	Victoria Falls	Victoria Falls
Niagara Falls	Rainbow Bridge	Natural Bridge	Great Barrier Reef	Great Barrier Reef
Iguaçu Falls	Giant Sequoias	Giant's Causeway	Harbour at Rio	Harbour at Rio

While no single place is on every list, the Grand Canyon is on four of the five and probably has the strongest case for inclusion.

Bailey includes at least one wonder from each of the six inhabited continents (and the Almanac list is almost identical). Certainly no part of the world is without some natural beauty. Since Mt. Everest and the Great Barrier Reef are easily the most famous features in Asia and Australia, it seems clear that the other lists that ignored these continents made major oversights. In fact, in both the Natural Bridge and View-Master lists, all but one or two wonders are American.

Perhaps the most obvious aspect of these lists is that they all include a waterfall (line 5). Lowell Thomas took an imbalanced approach and selected waterfalls as four of the seven wonders. Of the other lists, one selected Angel Falls—the world's highest. However, all of the others selected one of the world's most powerful falls; Iguaçu Falls in Brazil and Argentina is now known to be the most powerful of all when it reaches its peak flow. The *World Almanac* probably chose Victoria Falls because it is the most famous site in Africa, though it is far less powerful than either Iguaçu or Niagara.

The Serengeti, however, is equally famous in Africa and has no rival either among the plains of the world or among the large mammal ecosystems. In fact, Hillman Travel selected the Serengeti as one of only two natural wonders (the other is the Grand Canyon) on its list of Seven Wonders (see page 131).

Notice on the third line of the chart that every list has a volcanic feature. The Valley of 10,000 Smokes and Paricutin were eruptions during this century but are now outdated and surpassed by Surtsey in Iceland. Thus, Iceland is chosen in this book as the most amazing feature of Europe. Two lists also recognize a geyser, but the map addresses the geyser category by including Iceland.

The second line shows that three lists include a cave, but all fail to identify "the Everest" of all caves—Mammoth Cave—which is by far the longest. Two lists also recognize a natural bridge or arch rock formation. These are easily the most beautiful type of rock formation, but few would select an arch in place of the seven features listed on the chapter opener map. The record arch is Rainbow Bridge and would be an eighth wonder if it could be included.

Among all the world's features, five stand in a class by themselves for size: the Grand Canyon, the Great Barrier Reef, Mt. Everest, Mammoth Cave, and Iguaçu Falls. Furthermore, the Serengeti Plain features the most land animals, and Iceland boasts the greatest variety of volcanic and thermal features. These natural wonders represent seven types of landforms and all six of the inhabited continents.

All God's creations reflect His character, but these seven stand out as wonders of the world. God's creation displays His eternal power and Godhead: "For the invisible things of him from the creation of the world are clearly seen, being understood by the things that are made, even his eternal power and Godhead; so that they are without excuse" (Rom. 1:20). God's power is obvious in the majesty of the Grand Canyon, the roar of Iguaçu Falls, and the power of Iceland's volcanoes. In addition to grandeur and power, God is the God of order and beauty, complexity of detail, and vast knowledge. His beauty and order show in the Great Barrier Reef and the Serengeti Plain. Besides the beautiful setting, the life cycles and food chains of the many creatures in these havens for wildlife testify to God's orderly creation. His knowledge also surpasses the mysterious depths of Mammoth Cave.

"The heavens declare the glory of God; and the firmament sheweth his handywork" (Ps. 19:1).

THE GRAND CANYON, AZ, USA

Brown, muddy water splashed high in front of the small boat, blocking the view. Another wave crashed over them and filled the *Emma Dean,* which was flying its American flag with thirty-seven stars. Swirled around by a whirlpool, the boat went backwards through the rapid. Major John Wesley Powell and his men survived Sockdolager (meaning "knock-out punch") Rapids, but Grapevine Rapids ahead looked worse. The steep walls of the uncharted Grand Canyon boxed them in. Paddling to the side and clinging to the sheer cliffs, they tied ropes to their boats and floated them unladen through the rapid. Night came before they finished, and they slept fitfully, huddled on narrow ledges above the frothing torrent.

The next morning, beyond the rapids, Powell took stock. On May 24, 1869, ten men had launched from Green River, Wyoming, to be the first to explore the rivers. Flaming Gorge and Lodore Canyon had been rough. One of their four boats, the *No Name,* had been dashed to pieces in Lodore Canyon. That incident had prompted Frank Goodman, the only Englishman of the expedition, to leave for safer adventures. The Green River had eventually led them to the Colorado River and easier going through Glen Canyon. It had taken a week to run the sixty miles through Marble Canyon, which is the beginning of Grand Canyon. They had named Vasey's Paradise (a waterfall) after a biologist friend, admired caves (now called Royal Arches and Triple Alcoves), and camped two days at the mouth of the Little Colorado River to study nearby Indian ruins. On August 13, they had entered Grand Canyon proper, the most difficult and least-known part of their nine-hundred-mile journey. After fifteen more miles, the five-mile stretch of Hance Rapids, Sockdolager Rapids, and Grapevine Rapids had been the hardest so far. They had eaten no meat for over a month, had been rationing food for just as long, and had only a few dried apples and enough flour for ten days.

The hunger and hardships reminded Powell of the American Civil War. Raised in New York, he had joined the Union army, where he became captain of an artillery company in the Battle of Shiloh, April 6-7, 1862. Confederate General Albert Sydney Johnston died driving back the Union forces, but after Union General Wallace died, reinforcements came for General Ulysses S. Grant to force a Confederate retreat. Many of the 10,700 Confederate and over 13,000 Union corpses mingled their blood in Bloody Pond. Powell survived but lost his right forearm. Though maimed, he was promoted to major.

Now Powell found himself battling for his life against the Grand Canyon. With severely rationed food, he could not explore inviting places such as Havasu Canyon. On August 25, 120 miles into the Grand Canyon, they used ropes to pass treacherous Lava Falls, only to come to a more difficult rapid three days later. Here, three disgruntled men departed on foot: Bill Dunn, O. G. Howland, and his brother Seneca. Indians killed all three men a few days later.

Powell's men abandoned the *Emma Dean* and rowed their other boats, *Maid of the Cañon* and *Kitty Clyde's Sister,* through

Separation Canyon. The billows surged over the little boats, and
the explorers held on for dear life. Powell, with only one arm,
narrowly escaped drowning. On August 30, at the mouth of the
Virgin River, a group of Mormon settlers told them that they
were only twenty miles from Callville. Six of the original ten
celebrated the first canyon run at Callville: John Wesley Powell,
his brother Walter, Jack Sumner, Billy Hawkins, Andy Hall, and
Sergeant George Bradley. The ninety-eight-day adventure had
ended.

Today people arrive by car and by air. Cars can stop at numerous viewpoints along the eastern portion of the South Rim,
as well as at Bright Angel Point, Cape Royal, and Point
Imperial on the North Rim. Dirt roads lead to a few other viewpoints. Cape Royal has the added attraction of a natural arch,
called Angel's Window. Airplane and helicopter tours leave
from Tusayan, Page, Williams, and even Las Vegas.

Tourists venturing beyond their cars to descend into the
canyon must exercise caution. Walking downhill is easy, but
returning to the top in desert temperatures can result in heat
exhaustion. Other tourists stray from the trail and get lost. The
park conducts about four hundred rescues of lost and exhausted
tourists each year. These tourists pay thousands of dollars in
rescue expenses and learn the hard way the grandness of the
Grand Canyon.

Most hikers descend to the river on the seven-mile South
Kaibab Trail (too steep for mules) but return on the nine-mile
Bright Angel Trail. The fourteen-mile North Kaibab Trail de-

Rafting the Colorado River through the Grand Canyon

scends the North
Rim from Bright
Angel Point and of-
fers views of the
four-hundred-foot
cascade of Roaring
Springs and 148-
foot-high Ribbon
Falls. A van service

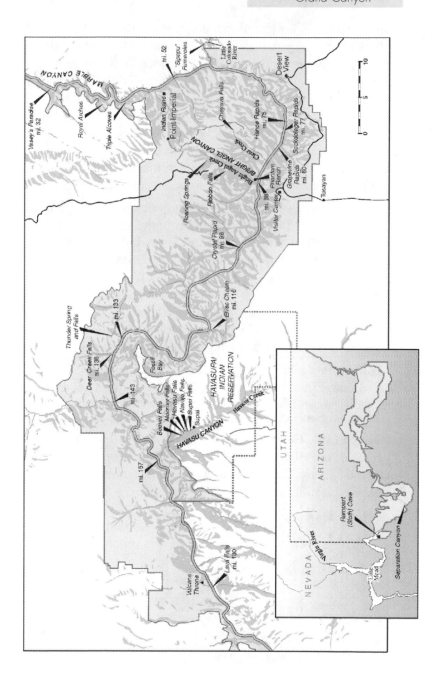

provides shuttles for rim-to-rim hikes. From the mouth of the Little Colorado River, backpackers can hike 116 miles to Elves Chasm by combining the nine-mile Beamer Trail, fifteen-mile Escalante Route, and ninety-two-mile Tonto Trail. Trails also lead to Thunder Spring, Deer Creek Falls, and Vulcans Throne, a cinder cone near Toroweap Overlook. The Clear Creek Trail leads nine miles to Clear Creek, where the most adventurous can bushwhack for four hours upstream to Cheyava Falls. Cheyava Falls drops eight hundred feet, making it the highest waterfall in Arizona, but it dries up in the summer.

Other outdoor sports include riding, rafting, and rappelling. Mule trips descend into the canyon from the visitor center via Bright Angel Trail. Riders cross the Colorado River at the bottom on a footbridge to reach their lodging at Phantom Ranch. The best raft trips (with or without motors for two to eighteen days) depart from Lee's Ferry and run the whole canyon, exploring all the falls, niches, and ruins. Rappellers may enjoy the Royal Arch Route and a hike to the pools, falls, and natural bridge at Elves Chasm involving a twenty-foot rappel.

Water plays a primary role in the Grand Canyon. First, water was essential for canyon Indians. The Hopi Indians believed that their ancestors emerged from the underworld through a spring called Sipapu, which bubbles out of a travertine dome along the Little Colorado River. The Havasupai Indians, or "People of the Blue Green Waters," have a reservation along beautiful Havasu Canyon, with its travertine-rimmed pools of sparkling-clean turquoise water. Visitors drive a dirt road to

Travertine pools below Havasu Falls

Hualapai Hilltop and then hike eight miles to lodging by reservation at the Indian village Supai. The hike to the campground three miles farther passes Supai Falls (twenty feet), Navajo Falls (sixty feet), and beautiful Havasu Falls (one hundred feet). A half-mile beyond the campground, hikers use ledges, tunnels, and chains to descend to the base of 196-foot Mooney Falls and continue six miles farther to the Colorado River via Beaver Falls (thirty feet).

The South Rim rises 4,500 feet above the river, while the North Rim soars 5,700 feet above the river. Some canyons are deeper: Hell's Canyon between Oregon and Idaho drops 7,900 feet to the Snake River, and Colca Canyon in Peru plunges over 8,500 feet. Though not the deepest, the mile-deep Grand Canyon is both the widest and the longest. It averages ten miles wide, reaches widths up to eighteen miles, and stretches 277 miles. The canyon area covers more than 2,000 square miles.

Grand Canyon, Arizona, which became a national park in 1919, may be the most famous natural feature in the world for its size, its beauty, and its significance. Along the rims, visitors can gaze across the vast gulf or glimpse the river a mile below. The canyon's colorful rocks, subdued by cloud shadows or highlighted by sunsets, display its grandeur unforgettably. The canyon area combines five of the seven life zones of the whole continent, so descending from nearby Mt. Humphreys to the bottom of the canyon takes one through the same ecosystems as driving from Mexican desert to Canadian tundra.

Evolutionists claim that the canyon also displays the greatest span of geologic history of any place on earth: two billion to 250 million years ago. They further claim that together with nearby Zion and Bryce Canyons, the entire geologic column is exposed. While Christians reject this view, knowing that the world and man were created during the same week, the Grand Canyon retains significance. Besides quite obviously displaying the power and glory of God, it also stands as a testimony to the truth of Noah's Flood. The sedimentary rock evidences that all that rock was laid down by water to a depth of about a mile. Furthermore, the layers in the rock evidence a typical flood deposition rather than sporadic deposits involving layer reversals through which the Colorado River slowly cut. The only reason evolutionists refuse to acknowledge this evidence is that the scale of the flood necessary to lay down rocks a mile deep at a five-thousand-foot elevation would have been worldwide!

In the Bible, God foretold that men would scoff at a world-wide flood and refuse to believe it (II Peter 3:3-6). Evolutionists today scoff, claiming that the canyon formed gradually. They choose to think that "all things continue as they were from the beginning of the creation" and "willingly are ignorant" that "the world that then was, being overflowed with water, perished." In verses 7-13, Peter says that the power that carved the grandest of canyons points toward another judgment to come.

MT. EVEREST, NEPAL AND CHINA

"Come back safely. Remember that. But get up if you can," urged John Hunt, leader of the British expedition. Hunt and the rest of the support team descended, leaving Edmund Hillary and five companions to doze fitfully in the two tents pitched at Camp 8 in the South Col. The South Col is a snowy ridge joining Lhotse and Mt. Everest, the fourth highest and the very highest mountains in the world.

The thin air at 25,800 feet caused altitude sickness and made all six men lightheaded and queasy. At dawn, one porter got so

Mt. Everest from the west

sick that he had to descend. George Lowe, Alfred Gregory, and Ang Nyima broke the trail. Following their ice trail, Edmund Hillary and Tenzing Norgay caught up by noon at the site of a battered tent. It had been the final Swiss camp the previous year.

Norgay had slept in it, but Hillary had not come this high. In fact, few people had been this high. The first climbs were permitted in 1920, and all previous attempts had failed. In those first eight attempts, seven from the north through Tibet and one from the south through Nepal, sixteen men had died.

John Hunt and his expedition had left Kathmandu on March 10, 1953, with 450 porters. They had transported fifteen tons of equipment for 188 miles to Base Camp at 17,900 feet. Using fifty porters, they had transported supplies to higher and higher camps. From Camp 4, George Lowe had worked eleven days establishing Camps 5, 6, and 7 on Lhotse before two other men had traversed to the South Col for Camp 8 on May 21. Five days later, two men had climbed toward the summit but attained

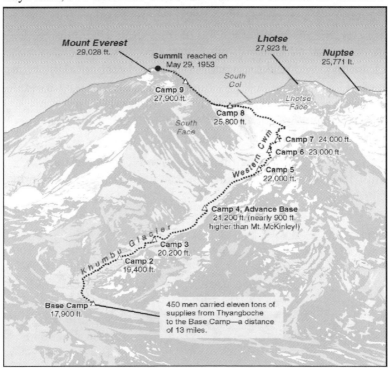

only South Peak (28,700 ft.). Though unsuccessful, they had beaten the old record by seven hundred feet, left supplies for Hillary, and reported conditions higher up.

That attempt had been two days ago. Now it was up to Hillary and Norgay. After a long day, the trailblazers descended, but Hillary and Norgay slept at Camp 9, a small ice patch at 27,900 feet, the highest camp in history.

Hillary and Norgay awoke at 4 A.M. and climbed for five hours to South Peak and the supplies the trailblazers had left three days earlier. Pushing on, they came to a sheer rock face forty feet high. To the left they looked down eight thousand feet into the icy, glacier-filled valley that they had been climbing for six weeks. To the right, a snowy cornice hung ten thousand feet above another valley. Hillary wedged himself between the rock and snow and shimmied up. They took half an hour to ascend the chimney.

At 11:30 A.M. on May 29, 1953, Edmund Hillary and Tenzing Norgay reached the top of the world. They rejoiced together and drank in their first unrestricted view of the vast range of unconquered peaks spreading out in all directions. Hillary removed his oxygen mask to sample the thin air and conserve bottled oxygen. He took pictures in every direction as proof of success, including one of Norgay waving four flags: the United Nations, Great Britain, Nepal, and India.

From 1953, when the first expedition reached the summit, until 1998, over seven hundred people have reached the summit

A village on a low ridge opposite Mt. Everest

of Mt. Everest. However, the death toll has also increased to over 150. In 1956 the Swiss climbed Mt. Everest twice and made the first climb of Lhotse. In 1963 a team from the

Mt. Everest from the summit of Kala Pattar

United States sent Whittaker to the summit as the first American climber, while Hornbein and Unsoeld became the first to scale the west ridge route to the top. Haston and Scott first ascended the southwest face in 1975, and in 1980 Ozaki and Shigehiro of a Japanese team first climbed the north face. On May 8, 1978, Reinhold Messner along with Peter Habeler became the first to climb it without oxygen, and on August 20, 1980, Messner became the first to reach the summit solo without oxygen. By 1998, two Sherpas had tied the record number of ascents at ten apiece: Ang Rita (age 50) and Appa Sherpa (age 38).

Mt. Everest has individual characteristics that are surpassed elsewhere in the world, but nowhere do all these features come together more dramatically. Mt. McKinley rises nineteen thousand feet from its lowland base, whereas Mt. Everest rises only twelve thousand feet above the Tibetan plateau. The Greenland icecap reaches colder temperatures than Mt. Everest, and several places including Antarctica have more spectacular glaciers. Atlantic gales buffeting the Scottish highlands and technical difficulties of mountains in the Alps match the winds and climbing conditions found on Mt. Everest. However, none of these other places combine all these factors at once: steepness, cold, glaciers, winds, and technical difficulties. In summer, the powder snows threaten climbers with avalanches, and in winter the gales are too strong to endure.

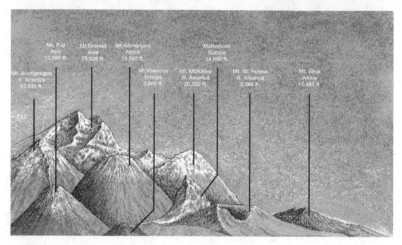

Moreover, these conditions are combined with the world's highest altitudes. Such high altitudes provide only one-third as much oxygen as necessary. Even a physically fit professional football or basketball star, if deposited at the top of Mt. Everest by helicopter, would become delirious within fifteen minutes from lack of oxygen. Mt. Everest, with its unequalled altitude, beauty, and glaciers, is clearly the most spectacular mountain in the world.

Mt. Everest, soaring 29,028 feet above sea level, straddles the international boundary between Nepal and China's province of Tibet. The Himalayas contain the ten highest mountains in the world: Everest, K2, Kanchenjunga, Lhotse, Makalu, Dhaulagiri, Manaslu, Cho Oyu, Nanga Parbat, and Annapurna. Even Annapurna rises 26,504 feet, while outside the Himalayas, the highest peak is Aconcagua in South America, only 22,835 feet in elevation. For contrast, Mt. McKinley, Alaska, at only 20,320 feet, is the highest in North America; Mt. Whitney, California, at 14,495, is the highest in the contiguous states.

In 1976 Nepal opened Sagarmatha National Park, using the Nepalese name for Mt. Everest. Besides the world's highest peak, the park also contains Lhotse, Cho Oyu, Ama Dablam, and many other nearby peaks. With airstrips near the park, visitors no longer walk from Kathmandu. The park gets about five thousand visitors annually, many of whom climb to Kala Pattar at 18,200 feet for a grand view of Mt. Everest.

SERENGETI PLAINS, TANZANIA

Bang! Teddy's shot rang out, and the blast from his elephant gun almost knocked him backward. He fired several more times until the great elephant paused and fell.

Theodore Roosevelt, his presidency completed, took a year's vacation in Africa and Europe and returned to the States in the summer of 1910. The highlight of the trip for Roosevelt was hunting on an African safari. Roosevelt and his son Kermit bagged about five hundred animals and birds, including seventeen lions. Roosevelt mounted a few of the animals for his Trophy (North) Room at Sagamore Hill, but he gave most of them to the National Museum at Washington, D.C.

In 1910 hunting was still legal and popular on the Serengeti Plain, but in 1951 Tanzania set aside the plains as Serengeti National Park. Today, all five of the famous African big-game animals are protected in the 5,700-square-mile park. Some 20,000 water buffalo, 2,000 lions, 1,000 elephants, and 100 rhinos roam the park together with an unestimated number of leopards. Including all the other types of animals, the Serengeti has more large land animals than any other place in the world. Furthermore, it is the only place left in the world where vast herds of large mammals still migrate. For these reasons, the park is the most famous national park in all of Africa.

Wildebeest migration on the Serengeti

Wildebeest migration is the central focus of the Serengeti. Since there are 1.5 million wildebeests, they impact the balance of nature throughout the park. The wildebeest, or gnu, looks ungainly and laughable, and seems to be made of spare parts. A wildebeest is a fast antelope with a mane and a tail like a horse, the beard of a goat, and horns like an ox. However, wildebeests are admirably fitted for the 1,000-mile annual migration. Though weighing up to four hundred pounds, they can still run 50 mph. During the rainy season, calves are born weighing forty pounds and are able to stand and run with the herd within minutes—an important ability for avoiding predators.

As the dry season approaches, the great wildebeest herds move north from the southern parts of the park. As they migrate, lions attack from the grasses, cheetahs from the rock outcroppings, and leopards from the scattered trees. Hyenas and wild dogs also prey on wildebeests. As the migration moves north, the herds cross rivers infested by huge, 1,000-pound crocodiles. Several hundred thousands of wildebeests die from predators, drownings, and tramplings before the herd reaches northern parts of the plain. Yet when the rains return, the wildebeests leave Kenya's Masai-Mara National Reserve and complete their loop back down to the south. The wildebeests multiply as God commanded them, and there are more births than deaths. God feeds the predators without disrupting His order.

Some 200,000 zebras live among the wildebeests and migrate with them. Many types of antelope also live on the plain, including 70,000 impala, 50,000 topis, 15,000 hartebeests (kongoni), and 10,000 elands. There are also roan antelope, waterbuck, reedbuck, bushbuck, klipspringers, duikers, the rare oryx, and the smallest of all antelopes, the dik-dik. Gazelle number a quarter million, mostly Thompson's gazelle but also including some Grant's gazelle. The 8,000 giraffes browse high in the acacia trees.

Hippos and crocodiles lounge in the pools along the river. Some 10,000 warthogs wallow in mudholes. Mongooses feed on insects, while baboons and monkeys inhabit the trees. Spitting cobras, puff adders, and the rock hyrax live among the rock outcroppings called kopjes (pronounced COP eez). At night, porcupines, ratels (honey badgers), and zorilles (striped polecats) become active.

Carnivores have a bountiful feast with all this wildlife. Cheetahs can pursue at speeds up to 70 mph, making them the fastest carnivores in the world. About 500 remain in the park. The 4,000 hyenas prey on wildebeest calves and smaller antelope or compete with the vultures for leftovers from lion kills. Foxes, jackals, and serval cats also inhabit the park. There is also at least one pack of up to twenty wild hunting dogs remaining. Wild dogs succeed in seven out of ten hunts, whereas lions succeed in only one out of three.

Of the many types of birds, there are 2,000 ostriches, the largest bird in the world. The kori bustard, the largest bird in the world

Hippos in the Mara River

King of the Serengeti

that is able to fly, also roams the plain. Secretary birds also strut across the plains, and flocks of flamingos feed from the small soda lakes. Storks and egrets wade in the streams. Six kinds of vultures and several kinds of eagles watch from the treetops. Scores of colorful songbirds flit everywhere.

The Serengeti is a large ecosystem that extends beyond the boundaries of Tanzania's national park. The plains spread from Lake Victoria to the Ngorongoro Highlands. Adjacent preserves include the Grumeti and Ikorongo Controlled Areas to the northwest, the Maswa Game Reserve to the southwest, and the Loliondo Controlled Area to the east. The Ngorongoro Conservation Area preserves the southeastern plain and the adjacent highlands. Kenya's Masai-Mara National Reserve protects the northern extreme of the wildebeest migration area.

The Ngorongoro Preserve is a favorite destination in its own right. Ngorongoro Crater, with its caldera ten miles across, is the main attraction. The crater has its own miniature ecosystem because the rugged crater walls make it extremely difficult for animals to enter or leave. The lake in the crater provides fresh water for most of the species of the neighboring Serengeti Plain, even hippos. However, the wildebeests and zebras of the crater migrate only short distances within the crater. From some places on the crater rim, visitors can see the majestic snowcapped peak of Mt. Kilimanjaro, Africa's highest peak.

The Serengeti has several problems. Since tribes along the

Rhino in Ngorongoro Crater

fringes of the plain, including the Masai and Wakuria, have doubled in size, they require more space for living and cattle. The poor national economy encourages some people to kill animals for food, but worse, it provokes others to kill animals for the black market, where wildebeest can be sold for meat, rhino for horns, and elephant for ivory tusks. Poachers use poison-tipped arrows, spears, snares, pits, or guns. Elephants and rhinos are the most endangered. The struggling economy makes it difficult to properly supply the rangers. At times, four rangers may confront thirty armed poachers. The brave rangers have made four hundred arrests in a single year and are making efforts to be good stewards of the Serengeti— the greatest wildlife preserve in the world.

IGUAÇU FALLS
BRAZIL AND ARGENTINA

Jungle! As far as the eye could see, jungle! Toucans flew through the lush forests, and monkeys chattered from the trees. The beautiful rain forest could have been anywhere in the Tropics, but the tapirs, coatimundis, ocelots, and jaguars re-minded Alvar that he was in South America.

Alvar Núñez Cabeza de Vaca had been born in Extremadera, Spain, about 1490. He had been on a four-hundred-man expedi-tion to Florida in 1528. Continuing to Texas, only about sixty men survived a shipwreck, and their numbers dwindled to less than fifteen after cap-ture by the Indians. After Cabeza de Vaca fled to Mexico look-ing for the fabled Golden Cities of Cibola, he eventually made his way to Mexico City and back to Spain in 1537.

Cabeza de Vaca had come to South America in 1541 because he had been appointed governor of the province of Rio de la Plata. From Santos on the coast near São Paulo, he had departed for Asunción. His progress had been good, and his thousand-mile journey was about two-thirds complete. He could not explain the faint but incessant roaring in the background. Could it be thunder?

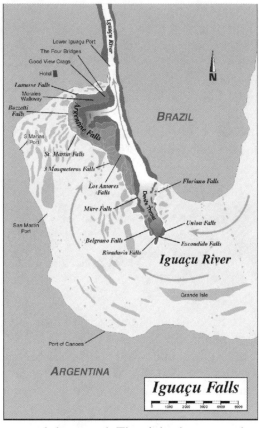

The stories of the local Indians drew Cabeza de Vaca toward the sound. The sight that greeted his eyes was pristine and immense, one of the seven wonders of creation and unsullied by people. He had discovered Iguaçu Falls. Later, he became governor of Asunción, was deposed by rebels, returned to Spain, and was banished to Africa. Eventually, he was allowed to return to Spain. However, until his death about 1560 in Seville, he did not forget the power of Iguaçu.

Iguaçu Falls (also spelled Iguassu or Iguazu) is the widest waterfall in the world with a crest about two miles long. This makes it four times wider than Niagara Falls! Iguaçu Falls is on the Iguaçu River, which divides Argentina from Brazil. Only fourteen miles downstream its water flows into the Paraná River, dividing Paraguay from Brazil.

rank waterfall	river	country	height	flow
1. Khone	Mekong	Cambodia-Laos	45	410,000
2. Niagara	Niagara	Canada-USA	182	212,000
3. Paulo Alfonso	São Francisco	Brazil	275	100,000
4. Uburupungá	Paraná	Brazil	40	97,000
5. Iguaçu	Iguaçu	Brazil-Argentina	269	62,000
6. Victoria	Zambezi	Zambia-Zimbabwe	355	38,000
7. Grand	Churchill	Canada	245	35,000
8. Cauvery	Cauvery	India	320	33,000
9. Rhine	Rhine	Switzerland	79	24,700
10. Kaieteur	Potaro	Guyana	822	23,400

The roar of Iguaçu Falls can be heard for miles, and the mist created by the thundering cataract rises so high that visitors can hardly see the falls. The waterflow averages 167,498 cubic feet per second (cfs) in the rainy season from November to March, though it drops off greatly in the dry season from August to October. The great variability makes for a low annual average of only 62,000 cfs, but during most rainy seasons the flow peaks at a level beyond the largest in the world. The falls have reached highs of 452,059 cfs, which is twice as powerful as Niagara.

At one time, Salto de Sete Quedas (Guairá Falls) on the Paraná was even more powerful, having a flow of 470,000 cfs. However, that falls is now flooded beneath the reservoir of Itaipu Dam. It was a spectacular cascading rapid, but few included it among the world's great falls.

Khone Falls and Uburupungá Falls, at less than fifty feet high, are rarely considered among the major falls of the world. Therefore, only two major falls exceed Iguaçu Falls in average annual flow. Of those two, Iguaçu Falls is roughly the same height as one of them (Paulo Alfonso) and much higher than the other (Niagara). Niagara Falls rarely reaches its natural average flow because of hydroelectric dams, and Paulo Alfonso Falls attains its natural average only in January because of an upstream dam that diverts water the rest of the year.

Islands along the brink of Iguaçu Falls divide it into distinct plunges. Niagara Falls has three plunges: the Horseshoe Falls,

177

Union Falls

the American Falls, and the Bridal Veil. In contrast, Iguaçu Falls divides into 275 separate falls. The highest is Union Falls at 269 feet. Other falls include San Martin and the Three Musketeers on the Argentine side, while Benjamin Constant and Floriano are on the Brazilian side.

Edmundo de Barros first envisioned a national park to protect the falls. He promoted this idea in 1897 using Yellowstone as his prototype. Brazil acted on his urging and created a park. Later, Argentina followed Brazil's example, and now national parks prohibit hunting on both sides.

In 1969 alone, two million tourists visited the parks. Most visitors arrive by air from Brazil's major cities. The town of Foz do Iguaçu serves as the tourist center for the falls and for Itaipu Dam. Tourists may fish, take safaris, boat to San Martin Island, ride rubber boats to the base of the falls, hike to the middle of Bozzetti Falls, or fly over the falls by helicopter. Trips to an island at the brink offer views down the mist-filled canyon of falls called the Devil's Throat. In fact, the wives of two

Aerial view of the Devil's Throat (left) and the Argentine Falls (right)

American presidents, on first beholding the indisputable wonder
of Iguaçu, have well expressed its grandeur. Bess Truman could
only exclaim "Poor Niagara!" Elizabeth Roosevelt stated, "This
cataract makes Niagara look like a kitchen faucet!"

GREAT BARRIER REEF

Valerie watched the huge manta ray building up speed.
Mantas look like birds with nine-foot wingspans as they swim
through the water. Abruptly, nose upward, it built up tremen-
dous speed and broke the surface of the water. Valerie observed
the great beast as it became temporarily airborne and then as it
belly-flopped on the surface. Valerie wondered whether the
slapping was to make sound signals to other mantas or to dis-
lodge parasites. Now the manta had spotted Valerie and glided
toward her. Although the little "horns" in front look dangerous,
Valerie knew that mantas use the specialized fins to fan plank-
ton into their wide mouths. Valerie swished her diving fins and
drifted closer to the ray. She scratched its underbelly, and the
manta relaxed and became limp like a pet dog. As they sank together to the bottom of the reef, the limp form settled over
Valerie like a blanket. Finally, Valerie got out from under her
manta blanket and looked around for her husband. Ron waved
to her and signalled to head back to the boat. Valerie waved as
the manta winged its
way into the dis-
tance, scattering a
school of yellow-
banded hussars in its
wake.

Manta ray in the Great Barrier Reef

As a husband and
wife diving team,
Valerie and Ron

Clownfish in anemone tentacles at the Great Barrier Reef

Taylor are among the world's foremost divers in the Great Barrier Reef, the most famous and beautiful coral reef in the world. The reef is also the greatest sanctuary for marine life in the world. With more film, Ron and Valerie returned to the world beneath the waves. Ron spotted on the bottom a guitarfish, which Australians call a shovelnose shark. Surrounded by Valerie and Ron, the guitarfish sent sand flying as it buried itself.

Colors swirled as the Taylors neared a coral island. Batfish, boxfish, butterflyfish, surgeonfish, trumpetfish, unicorn fish, zebra angelfish, and moorish idols scattered before them. Ron pointed at a large coral trout, and as Valerie neared she saw a small cleaner wrasse safely cleaning parasites from inside the trout's mouth. Nearby, they found harlequin tuskfish fighting for territorial rights and a parrotfish in search of algae crushing coral with its beak.

Ron and Valerie enjoyed searching out fish that hide. They saw clownfish cavort safely among the tentacles of stinging anemones, a blenny peeping from an abandoned shell, and squirrelfish huddled in a coral niche. Valerie remembered her friend Harry, a moray eel, that once let her draw it out of its hold and take it to the surface to show some children.

The underwater residents demonstrate many defense mechanisms. Fusiliers change color after dark. Groupers and black marlins lurk in the depths, eluding fishermen. Scorpionfish and stonefish blend in with the corals, awaiting their prey with poison spines. A lionfish moves majestically through the water, spreading its many poison-tipped fins. Stingrays glide by, armed with stingers on their tails. Barracudas, gray sharks, tiger sharks, and silvertip sharks prowl the waters fearlessly.

The Great Barrier Reef is home to fifteen hundred kinds of fish—more than any other place in the world. With twenty-three species of angelfish and forty-one species of butterflyfish, no other part of the world comes close to these records. Such totals could be repeated for almost any family of fishes. The reef also boasts unique species that live only in Australia—the scribbled angelfish, the Lord Howe coral fish, the Potato cod (which can reach 6.5 feet long and weigh 440 pounds), and the wobbegong, or carpet shark, with its camouflaged body and whiskered mouth.

Reef life also includes sponges, tube worms with their feather duster fans, and mollusks including squids, giant clams, conchs, and slug-like nudibranchs. The reef sports some five hundred species of these colorful nudibranchs—more than anywhere else in the world. Coelenterates, such as anemones and jellyfish, capture and eat fish with their stinging tentacles. The most deadly of the jellyfish is the sea wasp. Echinoderms of the reef such as starfish, sea urchins, and sea cucumbers seem harmless, but the crown of thorns starfish is poisonous and eats coral polyps. Crustaceans such as crabs and barnacles represent the reef's arthropods. Sea squirts (tunicates) squirt water when irritated. Reptiles include sea turtles, such as green and loggerhead turtles, and poisonous sea snakes. Herons, boobies, and other sea birds dive for fish. Mammals such as dolphins and humpback whales also play and spout in these waters.

Coral reefs form where limestone rock formations lie near the surface of the sea. Billions of living coral polyps live their lives attached to the rock. The four hundred species of polyps in the Great Barrier Reef

Lady Musgrave Island in the Great Barrier Reef

come in all colors, shapes, and sizes from less than an inch to over a foot long. As the polyps die, their skeletons sink and harden, forming a hard mass on which new polyps grow. The mass is hard enough to damage ships. When Captain Cook discovered the reef in 1770, his ship *Endeavor* ran aground on the coral.

The Great Barrier Reef is the largest reef in the world, stretching twelve hundred miles from Anchor Cay to Lady Elliot Island along the northeastern coast of Australia, a distance comparable to the distance spanned by the Great Wall of China. The reef is also more than fifty miles wide and covers seventy-five thousand square miles—about the size of Nebraska. Since the coral polyps are living creatures, the Great Barrier Reef is the world's largest structure made by living creatures.

Australia's world famous Great Barrier Reef Marine Park protects most of the reef and is the world's largest marine park. The park draws hundreds of thousands of visitors to the province of Queensland every year. Flights to nearby Brisbane make visiting convenient. Heron Island and Green Island are the most popular destinations for taking glass-bottomed boat tours, walking in tidal pools, snorkeling, and scuba diving. Many scuba divers enjoy exploring the shipwreck Yongola, and those seeking more remote places take a ten-day boat trip to the Ribbon Reefs.

The northern section of this most unique ocean ecosystem is still undeveloped and was recognized by an international marine council as one of the seven undersea wonders of the world (see Appendix 1). The Great Barrier Reef is certainly the most famous undersea wonder. It has the largest deposit of coral and a fascinating and amazing variety of life.

ICELAND

Dark smoke billowed up from the open sea. The fishermen
wondered if a boat had caught fire. The captain radioed
Iceland's coast guard, but they replied that no boats had sent out
a distress signal on this day, November 4, 1963. The captain approached through Atlantic waters near the Arctic Circle to in-
vestigate. As they drew closer, the fishermen could see that the
column of smoke was far too large for a ship fire. Vapor and ash
mixed with congealing lava chunks rose skyward. A volcano
was erupting beneath the sea. Just days later, the twelve-thou-
sand-foot column reached up to fifty-thousand feet. Soon lava,
piling up underwater, built up high enough to break through the
surface of the ocean. By November 16, the new island formed a
ridge 130 feet high and 1,800 feet long. By December 30, the
island expanded into a rounded shape 560 feet high. By March
the island covered one square mile.

Surtsey

Geysir

Such fountains of the great deep show God's power to transform the landscape cata-strophically. Within months, scientists had found bacteria, molds, seeds, a mussel, and a moth on the island. The volcano surprised evolutionary geologists who watched it develop because they expected these changes to take centuries. One wrote in *National Geographic,* "Despite the extreme youth of the growing island, we now encounter there a landscape so varied that it is almost beyond belief." God is able to silence the ignorance of foolish men. Now, twenty-five species of plants have been found, eighteen of which have es-tablished themselves. The sea sandwort is the most plentiful. Of the many types of birds that visit, six sea bird species nest on the island.

History bears record of other volcanic islands that have risen from the sea, but each sank back into the ocean depths. In fact, both Thera (Santorini) and Krakatoa are now undersea craters. Lava must harden to protect a new volcanic island from the pounding of the surf. Shield volcanos (*dyngas*) are rare in the world and occur primarily in Iceland and Hawaii. Iceland's other shield volcanoes (Kollotta Dynga, Skjaylbreidur, and Trolla Dynga) rise near Krafla and are extinct. Nowhere had people observed the birth of a shield volcano until Surtsey.

Iceland's 40,000 square miles, a region about half the size of the Great Barrier Reef, boasts one hundred volcanoes. Most of these rise from the central plateau and are stratovolcanoes rather than shield volcanoes. About twenty-five are active and display various forms including volcanic cones (Eyjafjallajökull), vol-canic ridges (Hekla), and explosion craters (Laki). These, to-gether with the land and marine shield volcanoes, give Iceland the record for the most kinds of volcanoes worldwide.

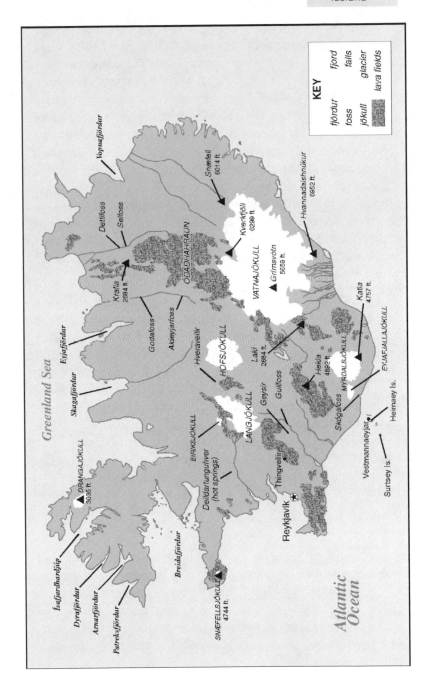

KEY

fjördur   fjord
foss   falls
jökull   glacier
        lava fields

Vopnafjördur

Snæfell
6014 ft

Hvannadalshnúkur
6952 ft

Dettifoss

Selfoss

Kverkfjöll
6299 ft

ÓDÁDHA-HRAUN

Grímsvötn
5659 ft

VATNAJÖKULL

Kratla
2684 ft

Katla
4757 ft

Godafoss

Alæyjarfoss

Hveravellir

HOFSJÖKULL

Laki
2684 ft

Hekla
4892 ft

EYJAFJALLAJÖKULL

Eyjafjördur

MYRDALSJÖKULL

Skagafjördur

Geysir

Gullfoss

Skógafoss

Greenland Sea

EIRIKSJÖKULL

LANGJÖKULL

Deildartunguhver
(hot springs)

Thingvellir

Vestmannaeyjar

Heimaey Is.

DRANGAJÖKULL
3035 ft

Reykjavik

Surtsey Is.

Ísafjurdhardjúp

Dyrafjördur

Arnarfjördur

Patreksfjördur

Breidafjördur

SNÆFELLSJÖKULL
4744 ft.

Atlantic
Ocean

Icelandic volcanoes have long been famed for their fury. Even the dormant cone of Snaefellsjökull inspired Jules Verne to pen *Journey to the Center of the Earth*. The eruption of Hekla in 1104 gave it a reputation as the gateway to hell for the rest of the Middle Ages. It erupted violently and continuously for thirteen months in 1947 and 1948, raining ash as far away as Finland. In 1991 it increased its recorded eruptions to seventeen. In 1362, the cone Oraefajökull (which includes Iceland's highest peak, Hvannadalshnúkur) erupted and became Europe's largest eruption since the destruction of Pompeii. When Laki erupted in 1783, the vapors killed half the cows and three-fourths of Iceland's sheep and horses, resulting in a famine that claimed ten thousand lives. Its lava flow covered 220 square miles, the largest in recorded histor; and a blue haze spread across Europe into Asia.

Lava fields from the volcanoes cover ten percent of Iceland. The largest lava field is Odadhahraun. The two types of lava are *apalhraun* or block lava and *helluhrawn* or ropy lava. Block lava is rough and difficult to walk on, whereas ropy lava can be smooth. These types are known to science as *aa* and *pahoehoe*, after their Hawaiian names. Another lava field, Hallmundarhraun, near Eiriksjökull, contains Iceland's longest lava cave, Surtshellir, about three-fourths of a mile long. *Fumaroles*, holes that emit sulphurous steam and fumes, are also common in the lava fields. Basalt columns similar to the famous Giant's Causeway in Ireland rise near Laki, and at Hraunfossar, there are full-fledged rivers that flow from the edge of the lava—some of the largest and clearest spring rivers in the world.

Iceland has over seven hundred hot springs, more than any other area worldwide. Hot springs vary in temperature from lukewarm to boiling. Boiling hot springs in muddy areas form cauldrons of bubbly ooze called mud pots. Iceland also boasts the largest hot spring in the world, Deildartunguhver. Its flows of 55 gallons per second could supply hot water for a town of thirty thousand.

Thirteen of the 250 hot spring areas are solfataras, or acidic hot springs, rather than alkaline. These occur only on the central plateau near active volcanic areas. The acids and minerals color the rocks to create beautiful hues magnified through the clear, calm pools. Most tourists visit the hot springs at Hveravellir. The most spectacular thermal feature is the geyser. Periodically subterranean forces shoot a jet of water from the geyser pool into the air. When the geyser is not erupting, the geyser pool looks like any other hot spring.

Hot spring in Iceland

Iceland, New Zealand, and Yellowstone comprise the world's three great geyser basins. Yellowstone has the most with two hundred geysers, and New Zealand set a record from 1902-1905 when Waimangu spouted daily to heights of a thousand feet. In Iceland, Geysir has drawn visitors for centuries—even before Waimangu and Yellowstone were discovered. Geysir's size and history make it the classic example of a geyser, and the term geyser is derived from it.

Iceland is called the "Land of Fire and Ice" because of its world record volcanic and glacial features. Vatnajökull, the largest glacier in Iceland, covers 3,100 square miles, which makes it larger than all the glaciers of continental Europe combined. Antarctica and Greenland have the largest glaciers called icesheets. The next largest glaciers are ice caps. Among ice caps, Austfonna and Vestfonna, both of which are located north of Norway in the Svalbard island group, exceed Vatnajökull in size. By comparison, the largest on the mainland of North

America is the Malaspina glacier, a piedmont glacier in Alaska and about half the size of Vatnajökull.

Vatnajökull, then, is the largest ice cap outside the arctic circle. It calves icebergs into a lake in the Grímsvötn crater, and its middle north lobe advances northward periodically. These glacial surges occur once each seventy to one hundred years and have been recorded since 1625. This longevity of records gives it the longest recorded surge history of any surging glacier. It also releases glacier floods (jökulhlaups) every five or ten years. Such floods occur when lakes under the ice formed by volcanic heat burst forth. Such a flood burst from Vatnajökull on November 5, 1996.

After Vatnajökull, Iceland's next largest ice caps are Langjökull and Hofsjökull, covering 390 and 375 square miles respectively. The fourth of the main ice caps, Mýrdalsjökull, covers 300 square miles and encompasses the volcano Katla. The 1918 eruption of Katla caused a record glacier flood which surpassed the water flow at the mouth of the Amazon.

Other glacier features include fjords and waterfalls. Fjords, glacier-carved valleys flooded by the sea, surround Iceland. The largest ones slice its north and west coasts. Waters from the glaciers also feed Iceland's rivers and waterfalls. The favorite tourist stop is powerful Gullfoss.

Iceland's record variety ranks it among the wonders of the world. While Yellowstone has more geysers, it has fewer hot springs and no ice caps or active volcanoes. Hawaii has active shield volcanoes, but it lacks geysers. Norway, New Zealand, Alaska, and Chile all have large glaciers and fjords world-famous for beauty, but they lack the variety of volcanic and thermal features. Iceland, though, not only is one of the three major geyser basins worldwide but also has the most hot springs, the largest recent lava flows, the widest variety of volcanoes, and the largest subpolar ice cap.

Most visitors fly to the capital city, Reykjavík, and take tours to Thingvellir National Park, a haven in the lava, which served as the site of parliament for nine hundred years. Most of these tours also visit Geysir and Gullfoss. Few visit the volcanic summits or ice caps, though views of them are provided on several tours.

MAMMOTH CAVE, KY, USA

Stephen Bishop rocked the ladder to check that it was firmly placed. The ladder spanned a yawning chasm called the Bottomless Pit deep in Mammoth Cave, and Bishop intended to cross it. Bishop, a black boy of seventeen years, was an adventurous tour guide. Though short in stature (five foot four), Bishop was lean and strong. His present customer wanted to see uncharted passages, and Bishop would not disappoint him.

Bishop scooted across the dark abyss to the opposite small ledge. On the far side, Bishop announced, "We are the first ever to cross the Bottomless Pit." After a pause, he added, "Let's explore." They pressed close to the wall and followed the ledge. They stepped across another narrow chasm and entered an oval passage. Soon the lowering ceiling required them to crouch as they sloshed along a muddy stream. They entered a huge chamber with several side passages. The little stream tumbled into a large river, the first major river discovered in Mammoth Cave, the River Styx.

Bishop had worked in the cave for only two months, but he had discovered more new rooms and passages than all the rest of the guides combined. Only about eight miles of passages were known, and

Exploring Mammoth Cave

all of those were large passages where walking was easy. People who ventured into the unknown were rare, especially unknown tight places, and no one ventured as often or as far as Bishop.

During the course of his years of exploration, Bishop discovered many of the spectacular formations and rooms of Mammoth Cave. Two years later, in 1840, he and another customer discovered Mammoth Dome. He discovered Echo River on his own, and he later rowed across with two adventurous tourists. They discovered the Snowball Room with its large gypsum flowers.

By this time, he was already an internationally famous cave explorer. His fame grew because he had explored more of Mammoth Cave than anyone else, and the seven different cave tours he arranged for visitors helped to promote the cave. Adventurers came from all over the country to tour the cave with this famous and knowledgeable guide. Scientists also sought him out for his knowledge of cave geology, which he had learned on his own by reading. He also spent two weeks drawing a beautiful map of the cave, the most detailed yet made. His reputation as cave expert soared further with the map's publication.

Bishop's map showed a river draining into Echo Lake, but the river was soon forgotten because entering the passage to go upriver was possible only at very low water in especially dry years. The river was rediscovered by Pete Hanson and Leo Hunt

Wild Cave Tour at Mammoth Cave

in 1938. They left their initials at the farthest point of their exploration upriver, and the passage was again forgotten for over thirty years.

Visitors today can still see the formations and evidence of Indian occupation known to Stephen Bishop. The cavern has a great variety of formations, besides the large stalagmites, stalactites, and columns. Visitors can see cave onyx, gypsum, flowstone, rimstone pools, draperies, and helictites, which twist and turn instead of hanging straight down. The most extensive Indian remains have been found in the Salts Cave portion. Flint arrowheads show that Indians explored deep into this cave. Bishop visited Salts Cave once, and he also found Indian remains at Gorin's Dome in Mammoth Cave.

Cave exploration is so popular that size records do not last long. The largest known cave room is in Sarawak Cave in Malaysia. Not too long ago, the Big Room at Carlsbad Caverns was considered the largest, but it now ranks ninth. The room in Sarawak Cave is three times larger. The deepest caves in the world are running a close race, also resulting in frequent changes: Huautla Cave in Mexico (4,067 feet deep), Pierre St. Martin Cave in Spain (4,334 feet deep), and Jean Bernard Cave in France (4,900 feet deep). However, Mammoth Cave is now by far the longest known cave system in the world. It will not be surpassed in the near future.

rank/name	cave location	length
1. Mammoth Cave	Kentucky, USA	350 miles
2. Optimisticeskaja	Ukraine	103 miles
3. Hölloch Cave	Switzerland	87 miles
4. Jewel Cave	South Dakota, USA	77 miles
5. Siebenhengste	Switzerland	66 miles

At first, the many entrances to the Mammoth Cave system were thought to be separate caves. Salts Cave was known to the Indians, and from 1871 to 1897, four entrances were found to Colossal Cave. Unknown Cave was discovered in 1903 and Crystal Cave in 1917. In 1955 Jack Lehrberger and Bill Austin discovered a passage linking Unknown Cave to Crystal Cave. Within the next six years, two additional explorations proved that all these caves were interconnected to form a twenty-one-mile long cave system in Flint Ridge. But the Flint Ridge Cave system was still thought to be separate from Mammoth. At that time, Mammoth Cave had forty-four miles of mapped passages

but had been recently surpassed as being the longest cave by
Hölloch Cave in Switzerland.

Exploration of Mammoth Cave		
year	length (miles)	history
—	-	used by Indians for centuries
1797	0	"discovery" by bear hunter Houchins
1812	2	saltpeter mining for War of 1812
1835	8	first map by E. F. Lee
1909	35	famous map made by Max Kaemper
1931	36	connection to Violet City entrance
1936	38	six entrances dug in twenty years
1956	44	exploration prohibited until 1969
1971	49	end of two-year survey
1972	58	before connection with Flint Ridge
1972	144	connection to Flint Ridge
1979	215	connection to Proctor Cave
1982	236	before connection to Roppel Cave
1983	294	connection to Roppel Cave
1999	350	end of century

Flint Ridge Cave explorers found passages leading under
Houchins Valley in 1964, which increased the cave's explored
length to thirty-three miles. The known length of Flint Ridge
Cave surpassed Mammoth Cave in 1967 at fifty miles and sur-
passed Hölloch Cave two years later. At sixty-two miles, Flint
Ridge Cave became the longest in the world. By 1972, Flint
Ridge had about eighty-three miles of passages, Hölloch had
seventy-two miles, and Mammoth remained third with fifty-
eight miles. Several expeditions in 1972 spearheaded by John
Wilcox culminated in the finding of Leo Hunt's initials at
Hanson's Lost River 5.5 miles from where they entered Flint
Ridge Cave. On September 9, Wilcox and his party of six ex-
plored far beyond the inscription and entered Echo Lake in
Mammoth Cave. (You can read detailed stories of these explo-
rations in *Great Adventurers of the Twentieth Century*, BJU
Press.)

The Flint-Mammoth Connection made in 1972 is the
"Everest of Caving," and the combined length of 144.5 miles
for the connected caves made Mammoth Cave the world's
longest. The length continued to increase as cavers found con-

nections with Proctor Cave and Roppel Cave. Some 329 miles of cave had been mapped by 1989.

Mammoth Cave became a national park in 1941. The eighty-two square miles do not include all the cave passages, some of which still lie beneath private land. With its constant temperature of fifty-four degrees throughout the year, sweaters or jackets are needed by the approximately two million visitors each year. This famous cave is located in central Kentucky just northeast of the city of Bowling Green.

Bridal Altar formation in Mammoth Cave

7 EPILOGUE

Christians may wonder why true wonders such as the temple of God at Jerusalem or the crossing of the Red Sea do not appear among the ancient wonders. While the exclusion of an event such as the parting of the Red Sea is understandable, locations in Jerusalem such as the temple could have qualified. Part of the problem is that the secular historians such as Antipater and Philo lacked spiritual insight. This epilogue identifies the seven spiritual wonders of the world, all seven of which are in Jerusalem, God's chosen city.

God promised through Moses that He would choose a place for His name (Deut. 12:5). God fulfilled His promise in the temple at Jerusalem, of which He said, "For now have I chosen and sanctified this house, that my name may be there for ever" (II Chron. 7:16). A city where God chose to reveal Himself is a wonder, but how much more wondrous that He chose it *forever*. There is no other city in the world that God chose for Himself. Jerusalem is unique: the most wondrous place of all.

God has revealed Himself in several ways. One way is through His Word, the Bible. Part of our Bible was written after the time of Christ, so only the Old Testament portion was known in ancient times. The oldest known copy of any portion of the Bible is the Dead Sea Scrolls, which are on display in Jerusalem. These ancient scrolls proved to the world that the copies that we have today are indeed accurate. They were not embellished over centuries by word of mouth. The modern copies are almost identical to the ancient Dead Sea Scrolls. Indeed, God wrote and preserved the Bible. The **Shrine of the Book** in Jerusalem displays the Isaiah scroll, part of God's revelation to man.

SEVEN WONDERS OF THE WORLD

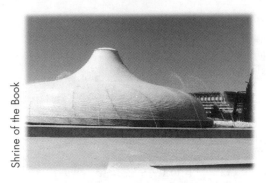

Shrine of the Book

God also chose to reveal Himself in a temple at Jerusalem. Solomon, the richest and wisest man in the world, finished building the splendid and beautiful Temple of God at Jerusalem around 955 B.C. It was so wondrous that even the Queen of Sheba came to see it.

So why is the Temple at Jerusalem absent from the list of ancient wonders of the world? The Babylonians destroyed the temple in 586 B.C. Though Zerubbabel rebuilt the temple in 516 B.C. and made it one-third larger, the older men who remembered the previous temple lamented. They did not mind the greater size, but they did not consider increased size important compared to important symbols of God's blessing. Besides a dearth of riches and gold furnishings, the new temple lacked the ark of the covenant, the urim and thummim, and the Shekinah Glory. However, the prophet Haggai, looking forward to the time when God in the flesh (Jesus Christ) would visit His temple, said that the glory of the new temple would exceed the glory of the old (Hag. 2:9).

Since the secular historians failed to understand the temple's spiritual character, it is no surprise that the fewer riches did not sufficiently impress them to include the temple of God at Jerusalem among the seven wonders of the world. A few ancient Christian writers, such as Gregory, included the temple of God (replacing either the statue of Zeus or the temple of Diana), but they alone understood its importance as the only temple of the true and living God.

About 12 B.C., Herod the Great repaired and expanded the temple so extensively that archaeologists often refer to it as Herod's temple. During Jesus' life on earth, He told His disciples as they looked at the temple that not one stone would re-

196

main standing upon another.
Indeed, in A.D. 70 the Romans
destroyed the temple, and
later the Arabs built the Dome
of the Rock on top of the
ruins. While the Romans left
no stone standing, they left
some underground foundation
walls intact, and a small portion of Zerubbabel's temple
can still be seen today. The
foundation on the west, called
the Western Wall, is exposed
to view. More popularly
known as the **Wailing Wall,** it

The Wailing Wall

attracts Jews from all over the world to worship God, mourn the
destruction of the temple, and pray.

Worship at the temple of God, in symbolic fashion, taught
the Old Testament believers that a substitutionary blood offering
was necessary to obtain forgiveness of sins: "without shedding
of blood is no remission" (Heb. 9:22). However, the animal sacrifices symbolized a purer sacrifice to come. "For it is not possible that the blood of bulls and of goats should take away sins"
(Heb. 10:4, cf. Isa. 1:11), but instead the animal sacrifices symbolized the coming sacrifice of Jesus Christ (Heb. 9:11-14).

Jesus Christ lived a sinless life. In particular, at the **Garden
of Gethsemane** He suffered temptation but did not yield to it.
Judas had gone to betray Him to leaders who envied Him. Jesus
knew His arrest and death were at hand, though He had done
nothing illegal. He wept and prayed, "Father, if thou be willing,
remove this cup from me: nevertheless not my will, but thine,
be done" (Luke 22:42). He experienced emotional anguish, and
the temptation to avoid undeserved punishment was strong. Yet
He did not flee but waited for the arrival of His tormentors.
Jesus "was in all points tempted like as we are, yet without sin"
(Heb. 4:15). Though no one knows the exact spot where He

Garden of Gethsemane

kneeled to pray, it was somewhere on the lower slopes of the Mount of Olives (Mark 14:26) in a garden (John 18:1) called Gethsemane (Mark 14:32).

Jesus showed most completely that He was fully human in His death. He did not have only the appearance of a man (which angels sometimes imitate) and the emotions of a man (seen at Gethsemane), but He died as a man on the hill called Calvary

Garden Tomb

(Luke 23:33). The place called Calvary is also called **Golgotha,** meaning "the place of a skull" (Mark 15:22). Though guiltless, He suffered as no one has ever suffered. His "visage

Calvary or Golgotha, the Place of the Skull

was marred more than any man, and His form more than the sons of men" (Isa. 52:14). He was beaten and tortured until He was unrecognizable, and His death by crucifixion was the most agonizing death ever devised.

His dead human body was buried in a tomb nearby. The recently hewn and unused tomb belonged to a rich man (Matt. 27:60) and was located in a garden (John 19:41; 20:15). It also had a huge stone which could be rolled in front of the entrance to seal it shut (Mark 15:46; 16:3-4). The **Garden Tomb** at the site known as Gordon's Calvary matches this biblical description perfectly. A rock formation with the appearance of a skull (Golgotha) forms a cliff below a hill (Calvary) and is a short walk from a tomb in a region where evidence of a cultivated garden (vineyard) has been found. No human remains were found in the tomb, and the track along which the stone rolled is still evident.

Why did Jesus suffer so? He could have fled, or He could have called angels to remove Him from the cross. All people deserve to die, but why should Jesus die when He was guiltless? How could a loving God allow it? Only a guiltless man who did not deserve death for His own sin could pay the penalty of another. It is because He is a loving God that He made the sacrifice toward which the animal sacrifices had pointed. "But this man, after he had offered one sacrifice for sins for ever, sat down on the right hand of God" (Heb. 10:12). Since all people

Mount of Olives

deserve death, only an infinite being could pay the penalty of all men simultaneously. For this reason, it is essential that Jesus was not only human, but also fully God.

Jesus paid the penalty for our sins on the cross, and He proved that He had accomplished this fact with visible evidence. He rose from the grave after three days in the tomb. His resurrected body was seen by over five hundred people. The accounts were written while witnesses remained alive, and any false reports would have been denounced by those alive. Jesus showed those witnesses His new glorified body that would never die again. What a wonder for Jerusalem! Then Jesus ascended into heaven from the **Mount of Olives**, promising to return one day in glory (Acts 1:11-12).

When Jesus returns in glory to His temple, He will come through the **Eastern Gate** (or Golden Gate). Unbelievers have walled in the gate with stones so that no one can go through, but they do not believe that the glorified eternal body of Jesus is powerful beyond all that we can imagine and is not restricted by walls. He came to the disciples into a room completely shut (John 20:19). In the eternal city, New Jerusalem, "there shall be no more death, neither sorrow, nor crying, neither shall there be any more pain: for the former things are passed away" (Rev. 21:4).

These seven locations around Jerusalem show clearly that Jerusalem is a wonder of the world like no other. They direct our attention to our Lord and Savior Jesus Christ and the events that prove who He is. Those who reject the sacrificial offering of Christ for their sins will have to pay for their own—suffering eternal torment. "Whosoever was not found written in the book of life was cast into the lake of fire" (Rev. 20:15).

He died in agony, suffering our penalty. He wants you to accept the gift of eternal life.

"For God so loved the world, that he gave his only begotten Son, that whosoever believeth in him should not perish, but have everlasting life" (John 3:16).

"But God commendeth his love toward us, in that, while we were yet sinners, Christ died for us" (Romans 5:8).

Have you accepted Jesus as your Savior? Admit that you have sinned and that you deserve death, and ask God to forgive you. Simply pray:

"Lord, I acknowledge that I am a guilty sinner worthy of eternal punishment in hell. But Jesus died to take the punishment I deserve. Forgive my sin because Jesus took the penalty for me. I am sorry for my evil thoughts and deeds and need Jesus to help me change. Thank you for loving me. Thank you for dying for me. Thank you for giving me eternal life and an eternal home in heaven. Amen."

Eastern Gate

APPENDIX 1:
Other Famous Sevens

The Seven Continents

All seven continents have islands: Madagascar in Africa; Ross Island in Antarctica; Japan in Asia; Tasmania in Australia; Iceland and Ireland in Europe; Greenland and Cuba in North America; Tierra del Fuego and the Galápagos Islands in South America. The term Oceania (or Australasia) includes New Zealand and the Pacific island groups with Australia.

The Seven Summits

The seven summits are the highest peaks on each continent.

Peak	Nation, Continent	First Climbed	Elev.(feet)
Mt. Everest	China-Nepal, Asia	1953 (May 29)	29,028
Aconcagua	Argentina, S. America	1897	22,834
Mt. McKinley	U.S.A., N. America	1913 (June 23)	20,320
Mt. Kilimanjaro	Tanzania, Africa	1889	19,340
Mt. Elbrus	Russia, Europe	1874	18,510
Mt. Jaya	Indonesia, Oceania	1962	16,404
Vinson Massif	none, Antarctica	1966 (Dec. 18)	16,067

The Seven Seas

The *seven seas* is either a figure of speech or it distinguishes the Mediterranean region into seven seas: the Adriatic, Aegean, Black, Ionian, Ligurian, Tyrrhenian, and Mediterranean Seas (the last describes only the open southern stretches).

The Seven Underwater Wonders of the World

A panel from CEDAM (Conservation Education Diving Awareness Marine research) International nominated twenty sites and chose seven. The freshwater site in Russia offers variety. The last is not a specific location, and the Mariana Trench is notably absent.

Great Barrier Reef, northern portion, Australia

Waters around the Micronesian island of Belau, Belau

Galápagos Islands, Ecuador

Lake Baykal, Russia

Belize Barrier Reef, Belize

Ras Muhammad Reef and northern Red Sea

Deep ocean vents of the Pacific, Atlantic, and Indian Oceans

7 APPENDIX 2:
What About Such-And-Such?

All the places below are worth visiting. Exclusion from the seven wonders is based on the criteria discussed in the Introduction. The wonders are listed alphabetically, so the category of wonder appears in parentheses.

Angel Falls, Venezuela (natural)—This tallest waterfall in the world has little water power compared to Iguaçu or Niagara.

Blue Grotto, Island of Capri, Italy (natural)—This sea cave in the Tyrrhenian Sea is famous for its beauty and uniqueness. Visitors can take small boats to see the turquoise color of the waters caused by sunlight filtering through the water, but the cave is rather small and lacks formations.

Chartres Cathedral, Chartres, France (architectural)—The Gothic cathedral, fifty-five miles from Paris, was finished in 1260 except for the 377-foot spire of 1513 (though a spire also remains from a structure of 1130). In spite of 174 stained-glass windows and ten thousand figures, it fails to be either the largest or the classic cathedral.

Angel Falls

Christ the Redeemer, Rio de Janeiro, Brazil (technological)—Completed in 1931, the one hundred-foot statue of Christ stands on a two thousand four hundred-foot peak overlooking the city. Its pedestal is twenty-two feet high, and its outstretched arms span seventy-five feet. It was matched in size by the ancient Colossus of Rhodes.

Colosseum, Rome, Italy (archaeological)—Titus dedicated

Christ the Redeemer

the Colosseum in A.D. 80, too late for the first wonders of the world lists. However, later writers such as Gregory also excluded it. Though interesting (with its beast fights and mock naval battles in the flooded arena), its history offers no vanished culture or undeciphered script.

Dead Sea, Israel (natural)—This sea within the Great Rift Valley is the lowest land elevation on the earth. At 1,312 feet

Colosseum

below sea level, it is much lower than the lowest point in North America (Bad Water, Death Valley, California at 282 feet below sea level). The desolate places below sea level have never appeared among the seven wonders of the world.

Eiffel Tower, Paris, France (architectural)—Finished in 1889, it predates twentieth-century technological wonders. It attracts three million visitors annually. At 984 feet high it held the record for the world's highest structure for forty years. Nevertheless, ten buildings in five U.S. cities surpass one thousand feet. Canada's CN Tower almost doubles its height, removing any superlatives.

Empire State Building, New York City, New York, U.S.A. (technological)—Completed in 1931 within budget and on time, this 1,250-foot building remains a classic example of a skyscraper. It held the records for the highest building and structure for forty years. However, other skyscrapers set records before it, and many surpass it (see page 78).

Garden of the Gods, Colorado, U.S.A. (natural)—The park features beautiful rock formations framing Pikes Peak (14,110 feet). The formations are not as extensive or varied as those at Bryce Canyon, Utah, and there are over a dozen higher peaks in Colorado alone.

Giant's Causeway, Dunlace, Northern Ireland, United Kingdom (natural)—This region of basalt lava columns on the Irish coast is interesting, but it fails to be superlative in size (700 by 40 feet) or to be unique (similar to Devil's Postpile in California).

Golden Buddha, Bangkok, Thailand (architectural)—The 5.5-ton solid gold statue of Buddha at Traimitwitthayaram Temple was made in the fourteenth century and stands fifteen feet, nine inches high. Perhaps the most valuable statue today, it was surpassed by the Statue of Zeus and the golden calf in ancient times.

Golden Gate Bridge, California, U.S.A. (technological)—This classic bridge is surpassed by many others (see page 90).

Hawaii Volcanos National Park, Hawaii, U.S.A. (natural)—Kilauea offers the most convenient viewing of continuous volcanic activity. The park offers lava fields, lava tubes, dome volcanoes, craters, and cinder cones; but it lacks Iceland's unique combination of thermal features, such as geysers, boiling hot springs, and mud pots with glacial features.

Golden Buddha

Herculaneum, Italy (archaeological)—The city's demise is intriguing. Mt. Vesuvius erupted in A.D. 79, burying Pompeii and Herculaneum in lava. Excavations uncovered mundane Roman baths, houses, stores, statues, and paintings, but it is not elaborate with amphitheaters, palaces, or temples.

Kamakura Buddha, Japan (architectural)—The forty-two-foot statue of Buddha is far less valuable than the forty-foot statue of Zeus, adorned with gold and jewels fashioned by the ancient artists.

Knossos, Crete, Greece (archaeological)—Sir Arthur Evans used the legends of King Minos to find Knossos in 1900. Excavating the Kephala mound on Crete, he dated the foundations at 2500 B.C. (before Mycenae) and its destruction by fire at 1200 B.C. The twelve-acre palace with complex passages connecting one thousand five hundred rooms vindicated the legend of the labyrinth and the genius of its architect Daedalus. Scenes

on frescoes and ivory figurines verified the sacrificing of youths to bulls or minotaurs. In 1952 Michael Ventris deciphered tablets in a form of Greek older than classical Greek (Linear B). This proved that Crete was the first civilization in Europe and the earliest Western Civilization. Though Knossos contributed a legacy of Minoan culture to Western Civilization, little remains for visitors to see at the site.

KVLY-TV antenna, Blanchard, North Dakota, U.S.A. (technological)—At 2,063 feet high, this antenna is the tallest structure in the world. Built to withstand 70 mph winds by swaying ten feet, it required only thirty-three working days to build (with no casualties). Since it uses guy wires, it is not self-supported (freestanding). A higher

KVLY-TV antenna

antenna was built in Warsaw, Poland, in 1974, but it collapsed in 1991, leaving the KVLY antenna as the highest.

Leaning Tower of Pisa, Pisa, Italy (architectural)—The bell tower for the cathedral at Pisa, built in 1173, is famous solely because of its lean, which makes the height of the north side (184.5 ft.) three feet higher than its south side (181.5 ft.). The tower has a 52-foot diameter, 293 steps, and eight enclosed stories. The centers of its first and seventh

Leaning Tower of Pisa

floors deviate horizontally by 15 feet, a foot more than in 1900. The necessary reinforcements detract from the tower's unique claim to fame.

Masada, Israel (archaeological)—Jews defended this fortress city on a high plateau in a last stand against Roman siege ramps. The cisterns and storage rooms can be viewed. However, the siege ramp is the highlight since the palace portions do not seem majestic because the frescoes were removed to museums.

Mt. Fuji, Japan (natural)—This snowcapped peak, 12,388 feet above sea level, forms a perfect volcanic cone with a 2,000-foot crater. Its beauty is famous, but its height and glaciers pale next to Mt. Everest. It last erupted in 1707, so it is classified as inactive.

Mt. Rushmore, South Dakota, U.S.A. (technological)—In 1939 Lincoln Borglum, son of Gutzon Borglum, completed his father's monument to four presidents. Borglum and his workers carved from the mountain four sixty-foot heads portraying Washington, Jefferson, Lincoln, and Roosevelt. The technology is fascinating but minimal compared to Gateway Arch, and the nearby statue of Crazy Horse, under construction in 1998, will eventually surpass its size.

Motherland, Volgograd, Russia (technological)—The figure is 270 feet high, twice the size of the figures of the Statue of Liberty or Christ the Redeemer, making it the largest statue in the world. Designed in 1967 by Yevgeny Vuchetich, it commemorates the battle of Stalingrad. However, when the bases are included, Motherland (about 280 feet) is smaller than the Statue of Liberty (301 feet) and does not have the interior stairways. It also lacks acclaim as a classic.

Natural Bridge, Virginia, U.S.A. (natural)—Its fame preceded Rainbow Bridge by a century, but its 90-foot length and 215-foot height pale in comparison. Its span is surpassed by many in the Southwest and the Ozark and Cumberland Plateaus.

Niagara Falls, New York-Ontario, U.S.A.-Canada (natural)—The Niagara River drops up to 182 feet. Water surges over its Horseshoe Falls and American Falls together at 212,000 cubic feet per second (cfs). Niagara has the highest average annual flow but not the highest seasonal flow. Iguaçu Falls is far wider and becomes ten times more powerful in the rainy season.

Old Faithful, Yellowstone National Park, Wyoming, U.S.A.

Petra

(natural)—Eruptions every 65 minutes up to 170 feet make it the most famous now, but it is not the highest. Waimangu (New Zealand) topped 1,000 feet in 1902. Iceland's Geysir reached 200 feet for centuries, becoming the classic from which all others took their name (see also Yellowstone).

Petra, Jordan (archaeological)—In the ninth century B.C., Edomites (descendants of Esau) cut huge tombs and temples out of the sheer canyon walls in an easily defended narrow canyon. Mineral deposits tint the cliffs pink, explaining the nickname Rose Red City. By 300 B.C. the Nabataeans conquered the city (as Obadiah prophesied), and Romans conquered it in A.D. 106. It fell into ruin, reviving briefly during the twelfth-century Crusades. In 1812 Jakob Burckhardt discovered the ruins, and now tourists to the Ma'an region of Jordan can visit. Even ancient writers excluded it as a wonder of the world.

Petronas Towers, Kuala Lumpur, Malaysia (technological)—In 1997 Petronas took the tallest building record from Chicago's Sears Tower, which had held it for twenty-two years. Petronas uses a spire to top Sears by a few feet, and though beautiful, this slight margin limits its uniqueness. Neither is it classic.

Rainbow Bridge, Utah, U.S.A. (natural)—The classic example of a natural bridge at 290 feet high, it is the highest in the world. Its 278-foot span is surpassed by two others: Kolob Arch at Zion National Park (310-foot span, 230 feet high) and Landscape Arch at Arches National Park (306-foot span, 105 feet high).

Redwood trees, California, U.S.A. (natural)—These are the world's tallest trees and the classic big trees. However, redwoods boast only the greatest height of any tree. The largest in girth (greatest circumference) are the sequoias, also in California. Also, the knarled and twisted bristlecone pines of California, Nevada, and Utah are the oldest living things on earth (see Great Pyramid). The photogenic bristlecones evidence growth from the end of the Flood; the oldest specimen is the four thousand five hundred-year-old Methuselah tree. Redwoods and sequoias display greater size, beauty, and fame, but the conflicting claims show that none serves as the classic big tree.

Rainbow Bridge

SEVEN WONDERS
OF THE WORLD

Sahara Desert, North Africa (natural)–The largest desert in the world is not local since it crosses parts of eleven countries African: Egypt, Sudan, Chad, Niger, Libya, Tunisia, Algeria, Morocco, Mali, Mauritania, and Western Sahara. Though the classic desert, it is too vast to be a specific location. Its 3.5 million square miles make it larger than the entire continent of Australia. Its three thousand five hundred-mile length doubles or triples the length of the Great Barrier Reef and would be matched by the Great Wall of China only if the wall were straightened out. Neither the wall nor the reef approach its one thousand-mile width.

Sequoia National Park, California, U.S.A. (natural)—These Giant Sequoias are the largest in girth in the world (see Redwoods).

Statue of Liberty, New York City, U.S.A. (architectural)— Including the 150-foot base, the statue is the world's tallest, but without the base it is only about 150 feet high and far surpassed by Motherland. The ancient Colossus set a standard for statues not obviously outranked by modern statues.

Terra-Cotta Army, Xi'an, China (architectural)—These are the largest collection of life-sized statues in the world, discovered in 1974 by peasants digging a well. The eight thousand

Terra-Cotta Army

statues, each six feet high, form an army that has guarded the tomb of Emperor Qin Shi Huangdi since 250 B.C. The figures are perhaps superlative for sheer quantity but certainly not in stature. Similar figures exist at Beijing (Ming Dynasty tombs), including twenty-four pairs of elephants and other animals as well as a dozen 15-foot giant soldiers (mandarins).

Valley of Ten Thousand Smokes, Katmai National Park, Alaska, U.S.A. (natural)—Two-thirds of this park's volcanoes are active. Mount Katmai erupted June 6, 1912, in an eruption rivaling Krakatoa and leaving a 56-square-mile crater. Thousands of vents steamed for years, but by 1970 only a dozen persisted. The eruption magnitude and steam activity prompted its inclusion in the early 1900s, but little remains for viewing.

Victoria Falls, Zambia-Zimbabwe (natural)—This waterfall of the Zambezi River stands 355 feet high (almost twice the height of Niagara). It falls in several cataracts into a spectacular gorge at 38,000 cfs. Both Niagara Falls and Iguaçu Falls are five times more powerful.

Washington Monument, Washington, D.C., U.S.A. (architectural)—The monument, finished in 1884, is 555 feet high. A 70-second elevator trip and an 898-step iron staircase lead to an observation deck at the top. Gateway Arch surpasses it.

Yellowstone National Park, Yellowstone, Wyoming, U.S.A. (natural)—Yellowstone, one of three famous geyser basins worldwide, has 200 geysers—the most in any area. It has some hot springs and fumaroles but no active volcanoes, craters, cinder cones, lava tubes, or lava fields. Iceland contains all such features (see also Old Faithful).

Victoria Falls

APPENDIX 3:
Notes for Teachers

SEVEN WONDERS OF THE WORLD

The Seven Wonders of the World can be a helpful tool to teachers of history or geography. This book provides the background for teachers to add interesting detail on world-famous places to their classroom presentations. Other teachers will be glad for an enjoyable book that will build student interest in places they are learning about. Some teachers may wish to assign the book or portions of it as outside reading. The following chart will help teachers identify places in the BJU textbooks where this material will prove relevant.

Ancient Wonders	Heritage 6	World Studies	Geography	World History
Great Pyramid	pp. 32-33		pp. 532-33	pp. 28-33
Hanging Gardens	p. 64		p. 502	p. 42
Statue of Zeus (Jupiter)	Ch. 6		p. 564	p. 52
Temple of Diana (Artemis)	Ch. 6		p. 512	p. 52
Tomb of Mausolus	Ch. 6		p. 512	pp. 62, 69-70
Colossus of Rhodes	Ch. 6		p. 366	pp. 69-70
Pharos (lighthouse)	Ch. 6		p. 532	pp. 69-70
Technological Wonders				
English Channel Tunnel		pp. 298-99	p. 309	pp. 616-17
Panama Canal			p. 263	
Itaipu Dam		pp. 582-83	p. 290	pp. 624-25
Dutch Dikes		p. 173	p. 334	
CN Tower			p. 234	
Gateway Arch			pp. 179-80	pp. 473-75
Akashi-Kaikyo Bridge			p. 484	pp. 617-18
Archaeological Wonders				
Stonehenge			p. 308	p. 210
Great Zimbabwe	p. 209		p. 589	pp. 167-71
Mesa Verde			p. 200	p. 317
Chichén Itzá	p. 186		p. 254	p. 318
Easter Island			p. 628	pp. 8-9
Angkor Wat			p. 453	
Machu Picchu		pp. 152-53	p. 280	p. 318

Architectural Wonders				
Great Wall of China	p. 109	p. 350	p. 475	p. 156
Taj Mahal, Agra	Ch. 10	Ch. 13	p. 434	p. 166
Dome of the Rock	p. 259	p. 537	p. 527	pp. 138-42
St. Peter's Basilica		pp. 32, 37, 40	p. 362	pp. 285-86
Palace of Versailles		p. 224	p. 326	pp. 339-40
Neuschwanstein Castle			p. 342	pp. 341-43
Borobudur			p. 459	

Natural Wonders			
Grand Canyon			p. 206
Mt. Everest		p. 86	pp. 441-42
Serengeti Plain	Ch. 9	p. 110	p. 580
Iguaçu Falls			p. 290
Great Barrier Reef		pp. 268-69	p. 604
Iceland			pp. 321-22
Mammoth Cave			p. 149

Teachers will also find some valuable resource information on various wonders that are featured in the following issues of *National Geographic*:

Wonder of the World	*National Geographic* issue
Angkor Wat	May 1982, pp. 548-89
Borobudur	January 1983, pp. 126-42
Channel Tunnel	May 1994, pp. 37-47
Dutch Dikes	October 1986, pp. 526-37
Easter Island	March 1993, pp. 54-79; January 1962, pp. 90-117
Gateway Arch	November 1965, pp. 605-41 (esp. 607-19)
Grand Canyon	July 1978, pp. 2-51
Great Barrier Reef	May 1981, pp. 636-63; June 1973, pp. 727-42
Great Pyramid	April 1988, pp. 513-50
Iceland	May 1997, pp. 58-71; February 1987, pp. 184-215; May 1965, pp. 712-26
Iguaçu Falls	July 1926, pp. 29-59
Itaipu Dam	August 1982, pp. 240-69 (esp. 245-49)
Machu Picchu	March 1992, pp. 84-111
Mount Everest	November 1988, pp. 612-53; July 1954, pp. 1-64
Panama Canal	February 1978, pp. 278-94
Serengeti Plain	May 1986, pp. 560-601
Stonehenge	June 1960, pp. 846-66
Versailles	January 1925, pp. 49-62

Bibliography

Austin, Steven A. *Grand Canyon: Monument to Catastrophe.* Santee, Calif.: Institute for Creation Research, 1994.

Bailey, George. *The Niagara Falls Question and Answer Book.* Toronto, Ontario: Royal Specialty Sales, 1998. Page 5 lists the seven wonders of nature and specifically says that Niagara Falls is not among them (see p. 157).

Brucker, Roger and Richard Watson. *The Longest Cave.* New York: Alfred Knopf, 1976.

Caselli, Giovanni. *Wonders of the World.* New York: Dorling Kindersley, 1992. This children's book compares ancient wonders with modern places.

Castles Neuschwanstein and Hohenschwangau. Ostallgäu: Verlag Keinberger, n.d. Guidebook.

Clayton, Peter and Martin Price, eds. *The Seven Wonders of the Ancient World.* New York: Barnes and Noble, 1988. Note introduction and epilogue.

Clucas, Philip. *Wonders of the World.* New York: Colour Library Books Ltd., 1983. Has eight ancient, five Middle Ages, six modern, and sixteen natural wonders.

Cottrell, Leonard. *Wonders of the World.* New York: Rinehart, 1959. Includes the seven ancient wonders and the following modern wonders (see page 55): Empire State Building, Golden Gate Bridge, Grand Coulee Dam, U.S.; *Sputnik I*; Snowy River Hydroelectric plant, Australia; Calder Hall and Jodrell Bank Radio Telescope, England.

Encyclopaedia Americana. New York: Americana Corp., 1976. See entries on "Borobudur," "Chichén Itzá," "St. Peter's Basilica," "Stonehenge," and "Seven Wonders of the World."

Encyclopaedia Britannica. Chicago: Encyclopaedia Britannica, 1983. See articles "Geyser," "Glacier," "Easter Island," "Iguaçu Falls," "Mt. Everest," and "Volcanoes."

Gies, Joseph. *Wonders of the Modern World.* New York: Thomas Y. Crowell Company, 1966. Covers thirteen wonders: Delta Project, the Netherlands; Empire State Building, New York; Verrazano Narrows Bridge, New York; Aswan Dam, Egypt; Tokaido Line, Tokyo; Simplon Tunnel, Switzerland-Italy; Oroville Reservoir, California; *N.S. Savannah*; US Interstate highway system; Telstar Satellite System; Chicago Sewer System; Ford Engine Plant #2, Cleveland; Titan Missile site, Denver.

Halliburton, Richard. *Richard Halliburton's Complete Book of Marvels.* Indianapolis: Bobbs-Merrill, 1941. Covers fifty-eight sites.

Hammerton, J. A., ed. *Wonders of the Past.* New York: Wise and Co., 1937. Has seven ancient wonders, thirty-two cities, ten tombs, ten palaces, nine monuments, twenty-six temples, eleven architectural feats, and fourteen ancient crafts.

Heyerdahl, Thor. *Aku-aku.* Chicago: Rand McNally and Co., 1958.

Hillman Travel Wonders of the World. www.travelwonders.com. For their list of seven wonders, see p.131.

Honshu-Shikoku Bridge Authority. www.hsba.go.jp

Meier, Sid. *Civilization II.* Hunt Valley, Md.: Micro Prose Software, 1996. Many influential wonders selected for this game are not places. Even the ancient list is nonstandard. Ancient: Pyramids, Pharos, Colossus, Hanging Gardens, Oracle at Delphi, Great Wall of China, Library at Alexandria. Renaissance: works of Copernicus, Magellan, Marco Polo, Michelangelo, Shakespeare, King Richard, Sun Tzu. Industrial: Eiffel Tower, Statue of Liberty, works of Bach, Darwin, Newton, da Vinci, Adam Smith. Modern: Hoover Dam, Apollo Program, Manhattan Project, United Nations, SETI Program, Women's Suffrage, Cure for Cancer.

National Geographic magazine. See multiple entries in chart on p. 215.

Natural Bridge. *Welcome to Natural Bridge: Experience the Wonder of It All.* Natural Bridge, Va.: brochure, nd. Natural Bridge lists natural wonders (see p. 157).

Pope, Gregory T. "The Seven Wonders of the Modern World." *Popular Mechanics,* (Dec. 1995), 48-56. World panel of engineers chose seven modern wonders (see p. 56) based on technological advancements, difficulty, and long-term significance. Also lists seven under construction: Hong Kong Airport, Akashi-Kaikyo Bridge, Kansai Airport, Petronas Towers, Three Gorges Dam, Afro Tunnel, and Troll Gas Field.

Rashleigh, Edward C. *Among the Waterfalls of the World.* London: Jarrolds, 1935. See pp. 34-41 for Iguaçu Falls.

Roberts, David. "Splendour in the Jungle at Angkor." *The World's Last Mysteries,* Pleasantville, N.Y.: Reader's Digest, 1978, pp. 242-56. Articles cover many sites including all seven archaeological wonders.

Rooney, Dawn F. *Angkor: An Introduction to the Temples.* Hong Kong: The Guidebook Co., 1994.

"The Seven Underwater Wonders of the World" *National Geographic,*

March 1990 (in the Geographica column) np.

Silverberg, Robert. *The Seven Wonders of the Ancient World.* New York: Macmillan, 1970. Modern list in afterword of Silverberg of American Society of Civil Engineers survey (see p. 56): Panama Canal, Oakland Bay Bridge, Empire State Building, Grand Coulee Dam, Hoover Dam, Colorado River Aqueduct, and Chicago Sewer System. To the last three (p. 55), Silverberg prefers the Washington Monument, United Nations Building, and Statue of Christ.

Snelson, Deborah, ed. *Serengeti National Park.* Tanapa: African Wildlife Foundation, 1992.

Tagliapietra, Ron. *Great Adventurers of the Twentieth Century.* Greenville: BJU Press, 1998. Includes outdoor stories of the Serengeti (Selous, pp. 1-6); Easter Island (Heyerdahl, pp. 53-60); Mt. Everest (Hillary, pp. 73-80; Messner, pp. 188-197; Morrow, pp. 202-206); and Mammoth Cave (Wilcox, pp. 117-130).

Thomas, Lowell. *Seven Wonders of the World.* Garden City, N.Y.: Hanover House, 1956. Ancient, natural (p. 157), and modern (p. 55): Angkor Wat, Taj Mahal, St. Peter's Basilica, Empire State Building, Hoover Dam, Dome of the Rock, Leaning Tower of Pisa, Statue of Christ, Kamakura Buddha, Shibam.

Thorarinsson, Sigurdur. *Iceland.* Chicago: Rand McNally, 1959.

Ulshafer, Fred. "Eclipsed but not Surpassed." In *Falling Waters,* Winter 1995.

View-Master. *The Seven Wonders of the World.* Edited by Thomas Lowell. Portland, Oreg.: Sawyer's, 1962. View-Master packet with thirty-two-page booklet covers ancient, natural (p. 157), and modern (p. 55): Angkor Vat, Taj Mahal, Chartres Cathedral, Empire State Building, Grand Coulee Dam, Mount Rushmore, and Mackinac Bridge.

Westwood, Jennifer, ed. *The Atlas of Mysterious Places.* New York: Weidenfeld and Nicolson, 1987. Has seventeen sacred sites, seven symbolic landscapes, ten ancient cities, and five lost lands.

Wonders of the World. Stamford, Conn.: Longmeadow Press, 1995. Discusses one hundred man-made wonders of the world.

World Almanac and Book of Facts, 1995. Mahwah, N.J.: World Almanac, 1994. See p. 694 on English Channel Tunnel.

World Almanac and Book of Facts, 1996. Mahwah, N.J.: World Almanac Books, 1995. Page 555 presents ancient wonders, nature (see p. 157), and Middle Ages; this list has the Colosseum, catacombs at Alexandria, Great Wall of China, Stonehenge, Leaning Tower of

Pisa, Porcelain Tower of Nanking, and Mosque of Hagia Sophia.

World Book Encyclopedia. Chicago: World Book, Inc., 1994. See articles on "Seven Wonders of the Ancient World," "Pyramid," "Skyscrapers," "Grand Canyon National Park," "Great Barrier Reef," "Great Wall of China," "Iceland," "Panama Canal," "St. Peter's Basilica," "Stonehenge," "Versailles, Palace of," and "Volcano."

Wonders on the Web!

For further information on the seven wonders of the world, visit the BJU Press website. The Press maintains links to various websites dedicated to wonders selected for inclusion in this book. Many of these are the official sites for the location and will provide much additional information. Whether you are researching or browsing, enjoy the convenient links offered to the wonders at the following:

www.bjup.com/products/7wonders.asp

The following agencies and individuals have furnished materials to meet the visual needs of this book. We wish to express our gratitude to them for their important contribution.

Cover

Pyramid, Stonehenge: Corel Corporation; Taj Mahal, Grand Canyon, Gateway Arch: Digital Stock; Easter Island Statues: Photodisc, Inc.

Title Page

Corel Corporation

Ancient Wonders

Brian Johnson xiv; www.ArtToday.com 1, 6, 12, 13, 14 (top), 15 (all), 16, 18-22, 24-26, 27 (all), 28, 30, 32, 33; Corel Corporation 4, 9; Library of Congress 7, 17; Gene Fisher 8; Unusual Films 10, 14 (left)

Color Insert

Corel Corporation 35 (top), 38 (bottom), 42 (all), 46 (top), 48 (top), 50 (top); Digital Stock 35 (bottom), 40 (bottom), 41 (all), 43, 45 (all), 47, 50 (bottom); Itaipu Binacional 36 (top); Honshu-Shikoku Bridge Authority 36 (bottom); Photodisc, Inc. 37 (top), 38 (top), 39, 40 (top), 44 (all); Eurotunnel 37 (bottom); Argentina National Tourism Office 46 (bottom); Icelandic Tourist Board 48 (bottom); Mammoth Cave National Park 49 (bottom); Queensland Tourist and Travel Corporation 49 (top)

Technological Wonders

Brian Johnson 52, 61, 69, 86; Digital Stock 53, 79, 81; Eurotunnel 57, 58 (top), 59 (all); Precision Graphics 58 (bottom); National Archives 60, 63, 64; Inter-American Development Bank 62; Itaipu Binacional 65 (all), 66, 67; Waterland Neeltje Jans 68, 72; Netherlands Board of Tourism 70, 71; Corel 74 (top), 75, 76; Brad Carper 74 (bottom); Photodisc, Inc. 80; Bridge and Offshore Engineering Association 82, 85; Honshu-Shikoku Bridge Authority 84, 88

Archeological Wonders

Brian Johnson 92, 115; Photodisc, Inc. 93, 97, 99, 112, 113, 114, 126; www.ArtToday.com 96, 105 (top); Corel Corporation 98, 100 (all), 101, 102; Colorado Tourism Board 104, 106; Ron Tagliapietra 105 (bottom), 107; Mexican National Tourist Council 108, 109; Mexican Government Tourism Office 110, 111; Ken Jensen 118, 119, 120, 121, 122 (top); Inter-American Development Bank 122 (bottom), 124; John Wolsieffer 123; Embassy of Peru 125

Architectural Wonders

Brian Johnson 128, 139 (top); Digital Stock 129, 132, 134, 137 (top), 138 (all), 142 (bottom), 144 (bottom); Corel Corporation 133 (top), 135 (bottom), 136 (top), 137 (bottom), 141 (top), 145, 146 (all), 147, 148, 151; Samuel Yau 133 (bottom); Corbis/Dean Conger 135 (top), 136 (bottom); Unusual Films 139 (bottom), 141 (bottom); Photodisc, Inc. 140; BJU Press files 142 (top); Ed Richards 143; Ray Martin 144 (top); Worldwide Slides 147; Gail Johnson 149, 152; Kienberger 150

Natural Wonders

Brian Johnson 154, 163, 167, 176, 185; Corel Corporation 155, 160-162, 164, 166 (all), 168, 169, 171, 173, 174 (all); Jim Hargis 170; J.M. Pearson/BioFotos 172; Argentina National Tourism Office 175 (all), 178 (all), Queensland Tourist and Travel Corporation 179 (all), 180, 181; Ward's Natural Science Est., Inc. 183 (all); Icelandic Tourist Board 184, 187; National Park Service 189 (all), 190, 193

Epilogue

Ron Tagliapietra 196, 199, 200; Unusual Films 197; Brian Smith 198 (all), 201

Appendices

BJU Press files 204; Corel Corporation 205 (all), 210, 211, 213; Charity Jensen 207; KVLY TV 208; Digital Stock 209; Xinhua News Agency 212